# A REPORTER REFLECTS

# A REPORTER REFLECTS

Brian Duffy
with Tom Hazuka

Tampa, Florida

Published by Gatekeeper Press
7853 Gunn Hwy, Suite 209
Tampa, FL 33626
www.GatekeeperPress.com



Book and cover design by Jimmy J. Pack Jr.

ISBN (hardcover): 9781662941009
ISBN (paperback): 9781662941016
eISBN: 9781662941061

# PREFACE

Journalists are not special people at all, they just live at the edges of human experience and therefore often have a perspective on the human drama that is different from most people, but that is no big deal.

I first became a journalist because I love to read and to write, but once I started, I realized how much fun it is just plain finding out stuff. I think of journalists as unelected emissaries of the people, or *demos,* in a democracy. As Jefferson and Madison both said in different ways, a robust press is essential to the functioning of a robust democracy. Journalists are not elected like politicians, but those of us who believe the job is a meaningful one think that it's important to try to understand what's happening in the world—economic issues, political distress, military mayhem, or whatever—and then try to explain it as best we can.

This may seem to be a presumptuous business, but Madison and Jefferson were no fools, and I like to think that neither are most of us who choose to take up this (dare I say?) noble profession.

As a reporter and editor, I learned the trade the hard way, coming up from the bottom, as a cub reporter. I made more than my share of mistakes along the way. Some of those mistakes were embarrassingly obvious; others I learned from over time. I sought to make up for them when I became an editor and tried to pass along what I had learned to the journalists who worked for me in my various editing positions at *U.S. News & World Report, The Washington Post, The Wall Street Journal* and National Public Radio.

You can learn a lot from your peers. I was constantly impressed by the industry and intelligence of the young reporters with whom I worked. I also learned a lot, obviously, from those who were older and more experienced than I. A wise man who oversaw the first investigative project I ever did, with a great colleague and wonderful wordsmith named Carl Hiaasen, taught me the first big lesson I learned as a cub reporter: "Assume as little as possible."

That advice was usually the first thing I passed along to the people I worked with after leaving my first job, as a reporter at *The Miami Herald*. There were other lessons too, of course. One thing I learned from hard experience as both a reporter and editor is that when one has the choice of seeking to discover whether something has happened as a result of a conspiracy, or as a result of incompetence, the correct answer is almost always incompetence.

Such lessons helped me, I like to think, become a better editor than I was a reporter. I also learned an important lesson from one of my best editors, at *U.S. News & World Report.* He told me the difference between good editing and bad editing is the answer to the question: "Is it different or is it better?"

Some of what I have learned over the years is included in these pages. I hope and trust it is neither presumptuous nor politically correct. I leave it to you, however, to be the judge.

# THICK CLOUDS OF MEMORY

## APRIL 2014

The ambulance was parked outside our house, lights flashing. I did not want to go to the emergency room but my fiancée, Mary Beth, a smoker who refused to see a doctor about her own health problems and would later die of cancer, insisted. So I went, although I had only two small bumps on my belly.

In the emergency room, the doctor ordered an endoscopy. This is normally a straightforward procedure where a small camera is inserted in one's throat and threaded down to examine the contents and overall quality of the stomach. For such a procedure, general anesthesia is normally not needed, but in my case the doctor ordered general anesthesia.

When I woke up four days later, a different doctor told me I had had a stroke while in a coma.

Since then, as I have tried to reconstruct my life in these writings about my journalistic career, such as it was, I have felt myself clawing through thick clouds of memory, trying to recall things I wrote about and things that I did. Much has come back to me, slowly and in fragments. I was fortunate, I suppose. The stroke damaged my motor skills but did not affect my speech or my ability to think, so I am able to remember most of my life before I had the stroke, and to dictate those memories.

I went to see a neurologist recently and he told me that I may have not had one stroke, but multiple strokes. This seemed to call into question the entire diagnosis I had assumed since having had the stroke.

My reflections in this collection about my career and about my current situation as a resident of a nursing home in New York State are as complete and as authentic as I can make them. I am not claiming 100% veracity for anything in these pages, only the attempt to have sought such veracity.

By the way, the bumps on my belly turned out to be nothing serious.

# DO THE MATH

"There are three CNAs on the floor and there are fifty of you," my day's first aide said in a prickly, peremptory tone. "Do the math."

Since I've been in this nursing home, I have been doing the math, and I am here to tell you it just doesn't add up. In the arcane argot of elder care, a CNA is a nurse's aide—it stands for certified nursing assistant—and they are the infantry of elder care, the troops one calls on in crises or catastrophes when sheer numbers are required to do the job.

Later that day I was in bed and needed assistance once again. It was close to midnight, and I needed a urinal. A kindly aide came in and provided the necessary assistance and I was fine. I spoke to her about the difficulties we have been having since the pandemic struck. The fact that there are not enough aides to give me the two walks a day their own director of therapy says I must get if I am to learn to walk again after having a stroke some years back, or the fact that I have not had a shower in two weeks because there have not been enough aides to give me the shower.

I told this aide that I had been a journalist before I came to this facility, and I was thinking about writing about the problem.

"You should do it," she replied in a cheery tone. "It's affecting everyone. It's affecting us. It's affecting you. You should write about it."

So I am.

# DO WHAT MAKES YOU HAPPY

It was a warm summer night, and as usual my family decided to have dinner outside on the back patio. My dad was at the grill. He fancied himself something of a cook but in truth his culinary skills were limited to searing meat on a barbecue. But at this he was a master, and few things gave him greater pleasure.

I was in my last year of high school and much concerned about my future. What would I do with my life? I had been thinking, for some reason, about law school but I had heard someone say that the only people who went to law school were those who couldn't think of anything else to do.

I knew one thing about myself. From a very early age I loved reading, then I discovered I loved writing. Now I was wondering about the wisdom of law school.

As we passed the plates around, I blurted out the question: "Dad, what do you think I should do?"

My father forked a piece of perfectly rare steak into his mouth and replied, "Brian, just do what makes you happy."

To understand the provenance of this statement you have to understand a little bit about my dad. His friends said that three things about him struck you immediately. First, he was a very funny man. Second – or perhaps this should be first – he was a very kind man. And third – maybe this too should be first – he was a very smart man.

My dad had gone to a prestigious Jesuit high school in New York named Regis that admitted students only on a scholarship basis, which was the only way he could afford anything other than the local school in his Brooklyn neighborhood.

He wanted me to take the test for Regis and I did, but failed.

As to the kindness issue, perhaps this example might suffice. Once driving me home from baseball practice, he saw a man pushing a woman, who happened to have one arm in a cast. He immediately stopped the car, raced across the street and interposed himself between the man and the woman. For his trouble, the woman yelled at him to "Leave my man alone!" repeating it several times with increasing fury.

On the drive home he was very quiet. I never asked him about the incident but thought about it often growing up.

As to him being funny, the evidence was, shall we say, mixed. My father was wont to deliver his best bons mots in a mumbled undertone that prevented them from being heard distinctly, but once you had heard them you would collapse in laughter.

Once he was playing golf with a friend who took an enormous amount of time before hitting his drive. Exasperated, my father said, "C'mon, will you hit the damn ball? My clothes are going out of style!"

Long after that summer dinner on the patio, I would remember my father's words of advice as I became a journalist. I had always been concerned that being a reporter wouldn't pay me a living wage, but once I landed my first job at *The Miami Herald* something occurred to me that should have been obvious. If you're doing something you love, chances are you're going to be good at it.

I went on to a reporting job at a news magazine in Washington D.C., *U.S. News & World Report*. I was promoted successively over a period of years to various editorial posts until I was the magazine's top editor. In that job I was paid a very good salary, probably more than my father had earned in the insurance business.

I moved on to other jobs at *The Washington Post*, *The Wall Street Journal*, and National Public Radio. At times over the years, when I felt the vast tide of news beginning to overwhelm me and feared that I couldn't keep pace with events, I would remember that summer night in my backyard surrounded by my family as my father said, "Brian, do what makes you happy."

It was great advice, and to this day I give it to young reporters with whom I am privileged to work.

"Do what makes you happy," I tell them. "Everything else will follow."

# LIFE WITH THE GRIM REAPER

## NOVEMBER 21, 2019

I moved in with the Grim Reaper only because it was the last bed in the house. I did not know much about rehabilitation places or old age homes, but I knew a little. I had had a right thalamic stroke at age 60 and I was trying to come back from it. The first rehab place I went to was pretty small and run by doctors. The only thing I learned from that place was that you should never let doctors run anything. Period.

The therapy was excellent, however, and I liked my two therapists. I had to learn to walk again, and it wasn't going to be easy. I had broken my left leg in two places after I had the stroke. On top of that, I broke my right leg not long after I moved into this rehab place. I can add the two broken legs to a long catalog of broken bones that included broken hips (left and right), broken arm (right) and broken ribs (four). I hadn't intended it, but I was a walking physician's desk reference. Or I guess I should say, since I still wasn't walking, I was a just a physician's desk reference.

I learned the Grim Reaper's identity in the most routine way. I had started out on the rehab trail almost immediately after my stroke. The accommodations in the first place I landed were no great shakes, but at least I didn't have to room with a Grim Reaper. Our nurse was an industrious, wise-cracking woman who treated us with the same snide remarks we greeted her with. One morning when she brought in our breakfast, she said "Here's your breakfast, Reap."

I was in the bed closest to the door, and I asked her why she called him Reap.

"Because he has a Grim Reaper tattoo on him."

I had never seen the tattoo in question, but it was somewhere on his person and I didn't want to ask where. TMI, if you know what I mean.

The Grim Reaper business might have been funny if we were not in a place where most of the people were very sick and some were dying on a regular basis. This had happened in the first facility I was in. My roommate there suddenly

became sick in the night and was taken out by paramedics. He never came back. My second roommate got a bad cold on Good Friday. By Easter Sunday he was dead, and they left his body in the room for the long weekend. So for a several days I literally roomed with a dead man.

My next roommate thankfully did not meet an untimely end. He had been a janitor in the local high school. He had been a smoker and suffered from heart disease of some kind. That was only the start of a long list of things that were wrong with him. Anyway, he was a gentleman of modest ambition and even more modest accomplishment. He lasted several weeks before he too disappeared in the middle of the night. Something about "problems with his blood work." He did not come back either.

The Reaper and I had very different tastes. His ran to YouTube videos about snakes and large reptiles. Mine were largely documentaries about baseball and history. The Reaper was not what you would call a pleasant man. He had a short fuse and barked at the nurses and aides anytime they entered the room. Most of the nurses were women of color, some did not speak English well and some were getting on in age. But they were unfailingly nice. There was no reason to bark at them or treat them rudely.

I would have not minded all the commotion if it weren't for the fact that I had the lesser space of the two beds in the room. Reap had the window and I had the door. Even that wouldn't have been so bad, but the constant agitation with the nurses and aides had me constantly on edge. Our nurse came several times a day to ask the Reaper if he wanted to walk. In this place the only way out was literally to walk your way out. If you couldn't walk you couldn't leave. That was the rule.

The Reaper in other words, was apparently settling in for a long stay even though he had already been there for more than five years. That was his business, though, and I didn't plan on worrying about it. As for myself, I was determined to walk out of the place as soon as my legs would carry me.

Taking part in the daily physical therapy sessions and walking with the aides in the hallway was the best way of trying to do that. The Reaper could stay there as long as he wanted for all I cared, but I sure as hell wasn't planning to. A kindly therapist finally took pity on me and got me out of the Reaper's room. He ex-

plained to me that the room had been like "a revolving door" for the past six months or so.

The Reaper delighted in finding ever new ways to make his new roommates suffer. Well, I didn't feel like suffering, and I was sure tired of his snake and reptile videos. My move out of my second-floor digs with the Reaper into a solo room on the third floor was accomplished without much trouble. One morning I went out to therapy and then it was me who didn't come back.

# THE ENEMY IN OUR MIDST

## APRIL 4, 2020

It was not as if the barbarians were at the gate exactly. There was no throng of armor-suited men or raucous taunts from outside the building walls threatening imminent attack.

What there was, of course, was an invisible killer that was felling cops, firefighters, U.S. Navy sailors — tough guys in the bloom of youth.

We had been told for days that the virus preyed on the old and the frail and within the walls of our rehab complex there was an abundance of both. If the virus ever got in here, my belief was, it would rip through the place like a California wildfire.

In the end, of course, the virus did get in. A doctor making his rounds admitted to me that several of our older residents were infected and had been immediately quarantined. Those in critical condition were being moved to hospitals.

For those of us in medical facilities for one reason or another, COVID-19 is no joke. At a San Antonio, Texas nursing home, when the virus got in, 67 of the facility's 84 residents were infected, killing one. The same has happened in Washington state, Maryland and a score of other states.

According to the Centers for Disease Control and Prevention, more than 400 long-term care facilities nationwide now have residents who are infected with the coronavirus, an increase of 172% from 146 on March 23.

For us here in suburban New York, the virus has arrived and we are just going to have to find a way to live with it. The usual gathering spots in the building where residents meet to exchange gossip, the hallways or the gym, are closed. We are largely confined to our rooms.

This experience, however, has proved even worse than waiting for the virus to attack. Now that it is an enemy in our midst, it is not clear what we can do about it.

What we want, of course, is for the infected residents not to be a danger to the rest of us. That many sound awfully selfish, but after weeks and weeks of worry, all the rest of us want is a little peace of mind.

# PREPARATION

I flew out of Boston to embark on the longest and most lavish experience of my life to that point. I was a junior in college in 1975, going to study for a year in Switzerland, but I had done almost nothing to prepare myself for the adventure.

Years later, when I traveled to all corners of the world as a journalist, I would do my best to prepare myself for each trip. Although there are few ways to prepare oneself to cover a war that involves putting young children on the front lines, or wars involving competing religious zealots, I made my way to the battlefields of Iraq, the mountains of Afghanistan, the hovels of Haiti and the scrambled soils of the Middle East.

For each trip I would read extensively and study reports of those who had been there before me. I had gone to Switzerland with no preparation whatsoever, and I would not make the same mistake twice. To be fair, though, the first time was not really a mistake, and a devil-may-care attitude might be just fine for a college student. But as a reporter and editor, I was a professional with responsibilities and people who depended on me.

Being unprepared was simply not an option.

# IN A SILVER CLOUD TO PARIS
## 1976

The tires of the big car kissed the curb quietly, easing against it like a great ship coming aside an old seawall. I tried to climb in the front seat but noticed that the driver was on the wrong side of the vehicle and that he was gesturing for me and my friend to get in the back.

My new friend and I were hitchhiking from London to Paris and the big car that stopped for us was, amazingly enough, a Rolls Royce. And not just any old Rolls but a Silver Cloud. We climbed in the back as instructed and I noticed that the driver, whom I thought had been dressed in a blue suit, was actually wearing a chauffeur's uniform, including the *de rigueur* blue cap.

We sped down the coast to Dover, and after crossing the Channel we met an old friend of mine on the other side in Calais. He wore a navy blue greatcoat and looked like a seaman ready to ship out for foreign ports. Sitting in the back seat as we pulled up alongside him, the rear window sliding down silently, it was truly a *"Pardon me, would you have any Grey Poupon?"* moment.

My friend got in with us and we proceeded from Calais to Paris. The driver was bringing the car to his boss, who would be meeting his mistress for a long weekend at the swank George V Hotel, just off the Champs-Élysées.

This was heady business for a middle-class kid from Long Island. I was going to university in Switzerland, skiing in the Alps, coming from London where I had seen some plays with friends and was now going to Paris in a Rolls Royce.

Truth be told, my old friend and I were on our way back to school in Switzerland, but by the time we got there we learned that we had both been expelled for being absent without leave, so to speak.

The director of our study program, however, a nun, had overplayed her hand and exaggerated our offenses. We had, in fact, been away from school without permission for too many days. But the good sister had added a bunch of other crimes we did not commit, and I called her on it. Grudgingly, she withdrew the

letters ordering our expulsion from the program and we were allowed to return to our studies.

It was an amazing bit of good fortune and, with the trip to Paris in the back of the Silver Cloud with my old friend and my comely new companion, it capped the greatest year of our young lives.

How much better and sweeter could life be?

I hoped to soon find out.

# LION COUNTRY

When I first started driving a yellow cab in New York, I was close-minded. The map of New York I had in my head reminded me of an old map of the world I saw as a kid. The map showed Western Europe with most of the major cities and rivers depicted. The rest of the world was greens and browns, and if you looked closely, you'd see a little script in Latin that read, "*Hic Sunt Leones*." That meant, "Here are lions." In my mind, Manhattan was the world on that map and the outer boroughs were all lion country.

I had been born in Brooklyn and was raised on Long Island, so my perspective was that of a commuter. I knew only Manhattan, and really only one block in Manhattan, the block surrounding Penn Station and Madison Square Garden. I knew that commuters getting off the Amtrak and Long Island Railroad trains queued for cabs to take them to their addresses elsewhere in the city.

On my first day on the job, therefore, I headed straight to Penn Station. Amid the crush of commuters, I spied a man who seemed like a likely fare. He was moderately tall and had a kind face and a nice smile. He was dressed in an Amtrak trainman's uniform with his name stenciled above the breast pocket. The man climbed in the rear of my cab and seemed pleasant. The address he gave me was Lexington Avenue somewhere in the upper 90's. I knew Lexington Avenue but only the Lexington Avenue of Midtown.

As we headed north and the street numbers grew higher, the man grew increasingly talkative. Was I really sure I wanted to take him all the way home? It wasn't necessary, and the neighborhood wasn't too great.

"No problem," I said, "I'll take you wherever you're going."

Perhaps twenty minutes later, we arrived at an address. It was squarely in East Harlem. Now we were *really* in lion country. The man thanked me profusely and pulled two twenty-dollar bills from his Amtrak uniform. The fare was only eight dollars. I thanked him, and he told me to keep the change.

My second fare of the day was also outside Penn Station, a man wearing a suit that would have probably cost me five weeks of fat fares. He was heading downtown to the Financial District. When we arrived at an address somewhere below Wall Street, the man said he had only a twenty-dollar bill and could he run to his office to get change. The fare was less than five dollars, so I said, "Sure, why not?" As soon as he exited my cab, I realized I'd been had. What a sucker I was! I went to the front door of the building he had entered and saw a crowded lobby and a bank of elevators. So much for the goodness of human nature.

Driving a cab in New York, one meets all kinds. It was not just the cheapskates and the cons, or the rich and the poor. It was the good people and then people who are perhaps not quite so good.

I spent around ten months driving a cab, and it was one of the greatest experiences of my life. I would get up most days at four in the morning, jump on the IRT and take it downtown from my apartment on the East Side to Union Square. The garage of the cab company that I worked for was on Tenth Avenue below 14th Street. To get from Union Square to the garage, I usually walked or took the crosstown bus.

I kept this routine up until just before Christmas, when a young man laden with gift-wrapped presents got into my cab. Most New Yorkers don't know it, but their cabs are typically rigged out with what cabbies call "a hot seat-meter," which starts calculating the fare the minute someone sits down on the back seat.

The young Christmas shopper sat in my cab long enough to ring up a fare of 86 cents. He also happened to show up right at rush hour, when I needed to return the cab to my garage at the end of the day. Then he insisted on going to an address on the East Side – the opposite direction I had to go to bring my cab back.

Frustrated and more than a little bit angry, I told the man I would not take him to that address and he needed to exit my cab immediately. I also informed him that he owed me a buck for the 86-cent fare. The young man got out of the cab at Union Square and dropped most of the packages that he had been carrying. One that he did not drop however, looked to me to be a rather nice bottle of Cabernet.

As we confronted each other in the thick of rush hour traffic, I insisted that he pay the fare. He countered that he would not and uttered some choice words that

are not fit for repetition here. We had arrived at what I thought was a proverbial Mexican standoff until the man brandished the bottle at me like a baseball bat and swung for the fences. The bottle raked across my nose, and I sank to the pavement like a stone. Two Con Edison employees working in the sewer in Union Square witnessed the whole thing.

As I lay on the ground, two things happened. First, the two Con Ed guys brandished steel pipes and took off after the guy with the wine bottle. Second, a man in an expensive German sedan stopped his car and offered to help me. He explained that he was a doctor visiting from Connecticut and was in town Christmas shopping with his family.

By now I was bleeding freely from the gash on my nose. The doctor staunched the blood with something or other and insisted on driving me in his car with his family back to my taxi garage.

It is said that there are a million stories in the naked city, and this one launched my journalism career. I wrote about it in an op-ed in *The New York Daily News* and was paid $250. It was quite a while before I was paid again for something I wrote, but a seed was planted.

Hey, I realized, I can do this.

# CROESUS!

When I got to Miami to start my new career as a reporter, I had almost no money in my wallet, just my Mom's Visa card. I took the first apartment I could find, a grimy, ground-floor unit in Little Haiti with a loosey-goosey lock on the door, across from a defunct drive-in where hookers turned tricks at night in the apartment next to me.

I had not gone into journalism to get rich so I had few expectations on that score, but the day after I wrote my first story, I strode out my front door and down the street to the first yellow *Miami Herald* news box I could find, jammed in a quarter, and fished out a paper.

It took a few minutes to find my byline, but there it was. Suddenly, I was rich—rich as Croesus!

# HOW I ALMOST GOT FIRED

The call came into the city desk, like hundreds of others *The Miami Herald* got each week. This was a woman with a high-pitched, panicky voice, and she was alarmed at something she had seen. She had been sitting in one of the city's juvenile courtrooms, and seen a young man sentenced to serve time with adult criminals in a local detention facility. This was truly cause for alarm.

Somehow, the call got routed to me. Though I was not a reporter, just a summer intern, I took the call assuredly, listening to the woman and scribbling notes furiously. When I placed the receiver back in its cradle, I told an editor what the woman had called about.

"Good," the editor said. "Check it out."

I grabbed the phone book—this was well before the days of the Internet—and looked up the judge's chambers. I called him straight away, and to my great surprise got him on the phone. When I identified myself as a reporter for *The Miami Herald* the judge said promptly, "You know, I can't discuss anything that happened in my courtroom."

I was not yet a reporter, but I already had a reporter's cynicism. I would not be put off by this legal mumbo-jumbo. The woman had called about a problem involving a young man and I would get to the bottom of it. End of story.

Although it wasn't the end of the story, at least not for me. I wrote the story for the next day's paper and it appeared on the Metro front. My troubles were just beginning. Had I not been so stupid or cynical, I would have realized that what the judge had told me was true. He could not discuss anything that happened in his courtroom because the proceedings all involved juveniles, and their identities were protected by law.

I nevertheless wrote the story. I identified the young man and what happened to him. The next day, the top editor of the newspaper marched across the newsroom to my desk and complimented me on the story. I didn't know it then, but

my troubles were already getting deeper.

Unbeknownst to me, I had called the wrong judge. It happened that there were two judges with the same surname, and I called the wrong one. Also unbeknownst to me, the same top editor who marched across the newsroom to compliment me on my story, demanded of other editors that I be fired.

I had wanted to be a reporter for years. Now, on the threshold of actually becoming one, I was about to see my infant journalism career strangled in its cradle.

Jim Savage[1], a wise editor of pacific and post-ironic habit of mind, took me in hand and gave me the best advice I ever had.

"Brian," he said, "assume as little as possible."

Jim worked with a regular stable of reporters at the *Herald* far older and more seasoned than I, and I always felt like the rookie on the team, or maybe the batboy. Even so, Jim always had time to make me feel welcome, to reassure me that my work was worthy of his time and efforts, and I like to think that maybe, somehow it was.

In the jobs I would come to have over the next years and decades, after leaving Miami and moving to Washington, D.C., I would remember Jim's sage words and impart them to people who worked with me and for me.

Assume as little as possible. No truer words or better advice was ever given.

[1] The inveterate editor of investigations of all kinds at *The Miami Herald,* Jim has brought down crooked county commissioners, improvident prime ministers, unrepentant presidential candidates and all manner of miscreants and general bad guys.

# MISSED SHOWERS

The problem nursing homes have today, in the depths of this pandemic, is we just don't have the numbers. There are simply not enough aides to do what needs to be done. *The New York Times* recently had an impressive front-page story on nursing homes and fact that many seem to be overprescribing anti-psychotic drugs because they do not have enough staff to manage residents with severe dementia who need to be restrained.

The problem I have in the place where I live is less extreme. According to the director of therapy in this facility I am supposed to be getting two walks a day from the nurses' aides, but they do not have the aides to give me two walks on most days. I'm unable to walk by myself, so am confined to a wheelchair. I'm also supposed to be given two showers a week, on Wednesdays and Sunday nights, but for the past two weeks, they have had to skip the showers. I suffer from a severe scalp condition that requires a strong medicated shampoo, and when I do not get the showers, I wind up scratching my head to the point where it bleeds.

This is the problem of running a facility for aged and infirm individuals where the staff must contend with the possibility of becoming sick themselves with the coronavirus. If there's a solution to the problem I don't know what it might be, and neither does anyone else. There is an investigation being conducted in New York State, of our governor for allegedly concealing Covid deaths from hospitals in the state's nursing homes.

The real scandal isn't how many have died in the nursing homes, it is how many of us must live in them, particularly during a pandemic.

# WATERFRONT LOTS

After only barely surviving my summer internship at *The Miami Herald*, I was dispatched by the gods and demigods who ruled the newspaper's newsroom to its two-person bureau in Key West. I had wanted to write since high school and only pursued a career in journalism after my father told me in a kindly but somewhat dismissive manner to do "what you want to do."

I was doing what I wanted to do but until arriving in Miami, I had never imagined I would get to be a reporter in a real newsroom. As a paperboy delivering the Long Island daily *Newsday*, I read *The Washington Post* Watergate coverage each day sitting atop the stack of newspapers the route manager dropped at the top of my driveway and devouring the coverage before I actually started to deliver the papers.

Reporting is a somewhat peculiar pursuit. It gives one at once the feeling of inadequacy because the subject matter may be so arcane and antithetic to understanding, but it also gives one the feeling of possessing a small amount of influence because what one writes, after all, is read by millions of people, or at least thousands of them. At any rate, I was determined to make up for the mistake I had made during my internship, an outrageous if perhaps understandable rookie error, and Key West was going to be my ticket to doing that.

Driving down to America's southernmost city, I took the Overseas Highway that connects all the Keys and is reported to be America's most dangerous roadway. Perhaps it is so dangerous, I thought heading south, because it is so beautiful. On either side water stretches away to almost infinity. To the left as you head south you see the Atlantic and to the right is Florida Bay and the Keys' back country, home to some of the world's greatest game fishing, not that I am much of a fisherman.

I was driving a Chevrolet Vega, an underpowered piece of junk that put my heart in my mouth every time I passed a school bus, Winnebago, or whatever. The

highway has only two lanes and no shoulder, so when you pass, oncoming traffic comes straight at you and there's no place to go but into the drink. Needless to say, I took it slow since this was my maiden voyage, as it were.

The *Herald* bureau in Key West occupied a dumpy storefront office on Duval Street, the city's main drag. It had a plate glass window with big block lettering saying *Miami Herald* in gold letters. Anyone passing by could see the two wretches assigned to the place sitting behind their metal desks dressed in their Brooks' Brothers shirts and ties, hair combed neatly, banging away at their computers.

The work in the Key West bureau was divided quite simply: one person covered the city of Key West; the other person, me, covered the county of Monroe. Monroe County had been named for James Monroe, one of the signers of the Declaration of Independence. Monroe had trod the same hallowed ground as Madison and Jefferson, but somehow failed to match those paragons of patriotic virtue stride for stride. His political heirs in the Florida Keys were indisputably worthy of the man, not so much venal as given to various pursuits of the lesser vices, most notably greed and gluttony. Only the gluttony here was for a kind of consumption that had nothing to do with fine dining or vast amounts of food. It had to do with consumption of the delicate but exceedingly fragile resource of the Keys themselves, islands in the truest sense of the word, with sand-fringed beaches, palm trees, and gentle waves lapping at the shores.

As the person responsible for covering the Monroe County government, I had to cover both the county commission and the county zoning board. This involved following the worthy members of both bodies on their monthly treks up and down the Keys to afford residents ease of access to their meetings, meeting variously in the upper, lower, and middle Keys.

While attending one zoning board meeting, I unearthed in a dense stack of zoning department documents an odd reference to a water pipeline on a key where no one lived. The mysterious pipeline was being moved from one side of a lonely county road to the other. Why was the water pipeline being moved? I wondered. Who was the water for?

A supposedly knowledgeable official told me that the pipeline had to be moved because where it had been placed originally, on the west side of the county road, had been designated as a federal preserve for the American crocodile.

Now this was interesting. Here were the political heirs of the politically suspect James Monroe going out of their way to save a piece of tropical real estate for the lowly crocodile. Could this be so? Intrigued by the mystery, I kept digging. A bit more research revealed that the landowners on the east side of the county road, where the pipeline was to be relocated, had all retained the same large Florida law firm and the same politically well-connected engineering firm. In Florida, perhaps like nowhere else, two words go together with a peculiar passion and power, and they are the words "waterfront" and "lots." By moving the mysterious water pipeline from the west side of the county road to the east side, the zoning board had given the landowners on the east side of the road waterfront lots that were now developable.

Waterfront lots in Florida come with the heady sense of sudden vast sums of cash and this, I realized, was the reason for moving the mysterious pipeline from the west side of the road to the east side. But there was a hitch—in the Keys, it seemed, there was almost always a hitch.

The hitch in this case was the fact that just beneath the ocean on the east side of the key where the water pipeline was to be located, North Key Largo, was North America's only living coral reef. The reef attracted divers, snorkelers and boaters, not only from all over the United States, but from all over the world. It was hard for me to imagine at that juncture that James Monroe's political legatees in Monroe County might sacrifice the goose that laid the golden egg on this reef as part of a crass real estate deal, but I had underestimated Mr. Monroe's political heirs. That was exactly what was going on.

By now I had more than enough information about the shenanigans that seemed to be in the works for North Key Largo, the northernmost of the Florida Keys. I wrote a memo detailing the entire sad saga and it ended, happily, on the desk of Jim Savage in Miami—as it happened, the same wise man who had come to my rescue after I made my terrible error during my reporting internship up in Miami. The wise man assigned one of the *Herald*'s best reporters to work with me on the story. Carl Hiaasen was a gifted investigator and a wizard of a word-

smith who happened to be one of Florida's best-selling crime novelists. Together we would continue digging into the roguery that seemed set to take place in North Key Largo.

In the end, we published a three-part series of stories on North Key Largo. The first part ran on a Sunday morning, and Carl called me later that day from Tallahassee, the state capital. The governor, a good man named Bob Graham, who would not have known James Monroe from a gas station attendant, would be announcing that he was going to sue to stop the proposed real estate development on North Key Largo. In court, the governor and his attorneys eventually prevailed, and North Key Largo was saved from further development in perpetuity, which is, I guess, a fancy way of saying forever.

The good guys, for once, had won. Finally.

# GETTING MINE IN *THE MIAMI HERALD*

In August 1981, *The Miami Herald* published the first of a three-part series of stories on a corrupt real estate development on the Florida Keys. The series explored several major land development projects that had been proposed for a little-known area on the keys called North Key Largo. In all, the developments would have added more than 250,000 new residents to the fragile Key's ecosystem, stressing the already over-burdened infrastructure and complicating evacuation efforts in the event of hurricanes.

The principal focus of the investigation was a proposed 25,000-unit condominium project that would have been placed on the junction at County Road 905 and the old Overseas Highway. This is the biggest intersection in the northern keys and essential to any evacuation plan in the event of a hurricane.

The day after the first part of the series ran, I got a call from my boss in Miami telling me to get the next flight back to meet with the newspaper's editor, John McMullan. McMullan was *The Miami Herald's* top editor and being invited into his presence after a story was published was not necessarily a good sign. In other words, I was scared as hell.

On the flight north to Miami from Key West, I peered out the plane's window eager to see if the bulldozers had begun clearing the hardwood hammock on the proposed Bougainville building suite. As the tiny plane hammered its way north through the humid air, I spied a massive black jewfish patrolling offshore like an enemy submarine and a bullet-shaped bonefish browsing for breakfast in the flats.

I don't remember the cab ride from the airport to the *Herald* building on Biscayne Boulevard, but I do remember arriving on the 6th floor of the *Herald* building and stepping off the elevator. As usual, the receptionist desk was empty. Behind it were two glassed bookcases filled with trophies that editors and reporters had won dating back to possibly the Taft administration.

I groaned inwardly that if things went badly this morning, I would never have one of those trophies. As I walked across the *Herald* newsroom past the city desk and through a jumble of the reporters' desks, I felt that every eye in the newsroom was on me.

McMullan's office was a glassed-in box on the far side of the newsroom. I could see that the paper's top editors had gathered along the long table used for the daily news meeting. This was not going to be good. I stepped into the office quietly and no one looked at me. This was really not going to be good. I was informed that we were waiting for the arrival of a man named Walter Revell. Mr. Revell was a principal in the engineering firm assigned to oversee the development of all of the projects that we had written about in the series.

When he entered the room, I could see that Mr. Revell was a knot of tense energy verging on anger. He was clearly not happy. He started to talk and immediately dispelled any doubt on that score. Most of the reporting that we had done on the Keys land development focused on Bougainville. It was a $1 billion-plus investment, and I should mention, a major advertiser for the *Herald.*

As Mr. Revell spoke, it became clear that his problem was not with the main issue of the story – the development at Port Bougainville – but with a minor sidebar I had written about a boat dock on a private house on the Keys. Eventually, Mr. Revell finished talking and there was silence.

Mr. McMullan broke the silence with his trademark gravely rumble. "Well, Walter," he asked, standing up. "Were we wrong?"

The question hung in the air like an arrow in a tautly drawn bow. Long nervous seconds (for me anyway) passed before Mr. Revell said no, we were not wrong. McMullan sat down abruptly and ended the meeting.

For the second time, I had imagined my nascent news career being ruined before it really even started. Now, I was off the hook. My co-author, Carl Hiaasen, shot me a sly smile as if to say, "No sweat. We're done." I smiled back wanly. I would not soon get over this fright.

More than a year after the series on the Keys ran, I answered the phone on my desk in the *Herald* newsroom in Fort Lauderdale. To my surprise, it was Fritz Scharenberg, the principal investor in the Port Bougainville development. Since Carl's and my stories were published, the editorial board of the *Herald* had been

running a regular series criticizing these developments generally and Port Bougainville specifically.

Once he had assured himself that it was me on the line, Mr. Scharenberg said: "Mr. Duffy, I've been getting mine in the *Herald* every morning and I don't like it very much!"

It was a reference to the *Herald's* marketing ads that said: "I get mine in *The Miami Herald* every morning, do you?"

I briefly apologized to Mr. Scharenberg and hung up the phone. Recriminations, I supposed, could wait for some other time.

# ERNST THE CROCODILE

The UPS guy hefted the big package into our dumpy storefront office on Duval Street. "Package for Brian Duffy," the man said. I was not a catalogue shopper and had not ordered anything, certainly not something so large and unwieldy. But the man said it was for me.

He left the package on the floor. Neil Brown, my partner in *The Miami Herald* two-person Key West bureau, and I set about opening it. (Neil later became editor of the *St. Petersburg Times* and managing editor of *Congressional Quarterly.)* Out came the two-by-fours, then the thick pieces of corrugated cardboard. Eventually, the treasure within began to reveal itself: a photograph six feet or so long of what I assumed was an alligator.

That's weird, I thought. Who would send me a picture of an alligator, especially one so big and lifelike?

Then I saw the note that came with the package. It identified the beast in the photo as not an alligator, but a crocodile. The couple who sent it had just bought a home at the Ocean Reef Club in North Key Largo, the northernmost of the Florida Keys and one not often associated with the others because it is not connected to them by the Overseas Highway. They had moved to Ocean Reef, the man said, to be close to the crocodile refuge on North Key Largo.

They had read the stories Carl Hiaasen and I wrote about the refuge and moving a water pipeline to enable development on the island, and evidently figured that a life-size photo of a croc was the perfect gift for me. Reporters write stories about any number of subjects under the sun and have no idea whether they will find an audience. I guess I found at least an audience of two.

My wife was flying into Key West from Chicago, and I had no plans so I thought we might drive up to Ocean Reef to meet my new crocodile-loving friends. Ocean Reef is your basic playground for plutocrats, offering golf, tennis,

deep-sea fishing, even guided bonefish tours. Elsewhere in the Keys there was not a trace of interest in crocodiles or those who might love them. Driving up the Overseas Highway we saw ads for tanning products, tiki bars, tattoo parlors, shellfish stores, trinkets of every description, dive shops—but nothing about crocodiles.

When we got to Ocean Reef we met my new croc-loving friends. He was chair of the chemistry department at the University of Pittsburgh and had invented Mace, the self-defense spray used on attackers. (That explained the half-million-dollar home at Ocean Reef, I thought.) His wife was chair of the physics department at the University of Pittsburgh.

They told us they had adopted a crocodile. Around their tastefully decorated living room were photographs of a crocodile in various poses of relaxation and repose, displayed like photos of a favorite child.

Trying to be sociable, I asked if the croc had a name. The answer was as simple as it was surprising.

"Yes," the couple replied in unison. They shared a look and the wife continued, "We decided to call him Ernst."

"Why Ernst?" I asked.

"We named him for Max Ernst," the man said, "the great German artist."

Whether to be a good reporter or just to be sociable, I asked a follow-up question. "Why did you name him for Max Ernst?"

"Because he is so logical," he said.

"Well," I said, looking at my wife. "I guess that explains it."

# BOWLING
## JANUARY 26, 2020

A game we rehab inmates do from time to time is bowling. This is not bowling with one of those heavy balls you find in a bowling alley. Rather, we use an orange rubber ball about the same size as a real bowling ball. One of the girls from recreation sets up the pins in the appropriate triangular pattern at one end of the room and we begin.

A resident will be invited to the opposite end and asked to roll the ball towards the pins. The other day, I was seated at the end of the room near the pins. The lady on my left was talking to a younger woman on her left but I could hear the conversation plainly, without trying.

At the far end of the room a sweet looking old woman in a wheelchair placed the rubber ball on the floor between her legs and gave it a shove. The ball rolled straight and true, knocking down all the pins. Strike! The lady on my left began asking questions of the younger woman.

"Was I married?" the older woman said.

"Yes, but it was a long time ago," the younger woman replied.

"What did my husband do?"

"He was a lawyer."

"Did I have any children?"

"You know the answer to that."

"Yes, two. Right?"

"Yes, a boy and a girl. The girl comes to visit you."

"Yes, I know."

"She seems very nice."

"She is very nice. I just don't know what she wants from me."

"She just wants to make sure you're OK, that's all."

"Is that it?"

"Yes, I think so. I believe so."

"How old are you?" the older woman asked.

"I am in my 20's."

"Were you ever married?"

"Yes."

"Did you have a husband?"

"No. A wife," she said.

At the far end of the room a plain-faced woman with closed cropped hair rolled another ball. It went straight and true, another strike!

# MURDER AND MAYHEM AND A PARROT

In sunny South Florida back in the day, Fridays were best for knocking over banks. The FBI knew this and they had agents, in cars and heavily armed, all over the place ready for the bank robbers. What they weren't always ready for was the robbers' overwhelming firepower.

Almost 32 years ago today, two bank robbers in South Miami approached a local savings and loan, eager to clean out the week's cash receipts. Special Agent Ben Grogan, a 15-year veteran of the Bureau, was one of the agents waiting. Jerry Dove, a neophyte agent, with just a few years on the job, was another. Six more special agents rounded out the bank robbery detail. Before the morning was out, both agents Dove and Grogan would lose their lives in a spectacular gunfight with the two bank robbers.

I was a young reporter who happened to cover the army of federal agents that Washington had dispatched to South Florida to stem the epic tide of cocaine that had begun washing over the Florida peninsula and infecting the rest of the nation. Most days I enjoyed my job because I never knew exactly what I would be doing when I left for work in the morning.

When I learned of the shooting in South Miami, I was immediately worried. I had lots of friends in the Bureau and hoped that none of them were involved or worse. More immediately, I was worried about how I would learn enough about what had transpired and put it in the next day's paper in some form that made sense.

I ran into the usual stonewall. The investigation was still being conducted. Next of kin had not yet been notified. Therefore, no one would have any comment about anything, especially for a nosy young newspaper reporter.

Several minutes after I made a round of fruitless phone calls, the phone on my desk in the city room rang. I picked it up but didn't recognize the voice on the other end. The caller politely inquired if I was Brian Duffy and if I was writing

about the shooting involving the FBI agents and bank robbers in South Miami. I told him I was. He asked me if I had access to the car-to-car transmissions of the FBI agents involved in the incident. I told him that I did not, and hopefully asked if he might have such a tape. In fact, he said that he did.

The man evidently lived in a trailer somewhere west of Miami toward the Everglades, possibly in a rock pit. I never did meet him and to this day I have no idea who he is. He was kind enough to courier over to my office a copy of the tape. He asked for no money and declined to even identify himself. But the tape, for the purposes of a desperate young reporter at least, was a veritable gold mine. Not only was it broken down second by second, the sounds of the gun battle were unmistakable – and terrifying.

What I had not counted on, however, was the intrusion of a parrot on the recording. This kind gentleman caller who offered me this godsend tape, evidently made a habit of taping the car-to-car transmissions of all the federal agencies of Miami on a police scanner. The tape recorder he used was voice activated, but he forgot to worry about the presence of his parrot interfering with the recording.

In any case, amid the noise of bullets flying and men dying was the incongruous presence of a parrot cackling over the sounds of murder and mayhem. I did my best to ignore the parrot and managed to get my story on page one the next day.

They say God smiles on fools and drunks, but perhaps that should be amended to include desperate young reporters. Maybe it should also be amended to say that our good Lord is not without a sense of humor.

# FBI SOURCES

Anyone reading these reflections on my journalism career, such as it was, probably already knows that I was blessed with having very good FBI sources. For a reporter like me, who covered national security issues, this was not just a blessing but a necessity. The sources had not simply fallen into my lap; I had worked hard over the years to develop them, cultivate them, and earn their trust and respect.

In Miami I had covered the murder of two FBI agents, a young agent named Jerry Dove and a grizzled veteran named Ben Grogan. They had been working a bank robbery detail with other agents when they were shot to death by two heavily armed men trying to rob the bank they had been staking out.

The agents who died were very different. Jerry Dove was a young, clean-cut guy who probably took orders well and followed them to the letter. Grogan was a physical fitness buff who worked out religiously and was in excellent shape. The agents were murdered by two men with automatic weapons and a sawed-off shotgun. One agent, John Hancock, had only a five-shot revolver in an ankle holster, and though the others had stronger weaponry they were outgunned by the criminals.

I was fortunate enough to have been given by a source a tape recording of the car-to-car transmission of the FBI vehicles during the attack, and I shared it with FBI Director William Webster. Judge Webster, as I always addressed him, using his honorific from when he had sat on the bench, was grateful for having been given the tape, and I was told that it would later be used in FBI training films at the Bureau's academy in Quantico, Virginia.

After I moved to Washington D.C., I happened to be in the FBI's sprawling field office and met a young agent who showed up to report for duty. John O'Neill had just flown in from Chicago, where he had served as a special agent working white-collar crime cases. In Washington, O'Neill wished to cover terrorism cases.

Wow, I thought, this guy is going from the minor leagues straight to the World Series in a few short months. I'm going to have to get to know this agent and keep tabs on him.

It would not work out that way, however. O'Neill became a close friend of Richard A. Clarke, the National Security Advisor to President George W. Bush and later to President Clinton. According to Clarke, O'Neill was obsessed with al-Qaeda, the terrorist organization that reported to Osama Bin Laden. According to Clarke, O'Neill was a hard charger and it may have been his hard charging that ultimately got him in trouble, for the Bureau, which has a nasty habit of devouring its young, eventually charged O'Neill with mishandling classified information about al-Qaeda. This forced John into early retirement, and he took a job as director of security at the World Trade Center.

He was on the job there on the morning of September 11 when the two planes hit the Twin Towers. He did not survive, but his memory and, I hope, his dedication to protecting our country from terrorists like al-Qaeda outlive him. He was a good man and I regret not having gotten to know him.

# GIANNI VERSACE AND MY FBI SOURCE

The news bulletin tripped the buzzer on the wire service machine on the national desk where I happened to be sitting that night. One of the other editors glanced at the lede, looked up and said, "Looks like this is you, Duffy."

I peeked over the man's shoulder, saw the Miami dateline and realized he was right. I had only been at *The Washington Post* for a few weeks but had come there from *The Miami Herald*, where I had been a reporter.

The bulletin said that Gianni Versace, the iconic Italian fashion designer, had been murdered on the front steps of Casa Casuarina, his baronial Italian mansion in Miami Beach. This was big news in anyone's book, I thought.

Versace had made news not only in fashion but in business, art, real estate, you name it. Quickly, I thought about who I could call among my old Miami sources. Then I dialed a number I knew from memory. The man I was looking for wasn't there, I was told. He was in California, in San Francisco. I was given a number and called it immediately.

The man I was looking for picked up and I told him why I was calling.

"Yeah," the FBI man said. "A real tragedy, but we got the bastard who did it. Some mutt named Cunanan, a serial killer."

The name was unfamiliar to me so I wrote it phonetically on a legal pad. I looked up and told the other editors what I was getting. Andrew Philip Cunanan was a whip-thin gay white man in his late 20s who had murdered four people in three months before killing Versace.

When I finished reporting and writing the story my boss and I went across the street to the Madison Hotel. Over drinks, she asked me how well I had known my FBI source before calling him that night. She asked me other questions about him, what he was like and what type of cases he worked on.

As we walked out the hotel's front door into the cool, crisp night, she asked me one last question. "Has he ever given you any wrong information?"

I turned as I headed toward my car.

"Only once or twice," I said.

# DOWNRIGHT CACOPHONOUS

## MARCH 22, 2020

Some days it's as quiet as a cave in here. On other days the noise, if not quite deafening, is downright cacophonous. The other day was one such day.

Across the hall from me is a diminutive Asian man who may be either Bangladeshi or Pakistani, but I am no expert.

From his room came sounds that could only be described as an argument. One of the aides on our floor who is built like a bulldozer and has just as much empathy was interrogating the man.

"I want to know who gave you all these towels," she said, repeating the question several times after evidently getting no answer.

After a moment she stepped into the hallway and said in a loud voice to no one in particular: "I want to know who gave him all those towels."

Had she asked me I could have told her that no one gave him the towels and that he was simply a towel thief.

Every day between 3 and 4 p.m., the man rolled his wheelchair to the laundry cart that parked just outside my room. The cart was covered by a canvas shroud secured by Velcro strips. The man would push his pathetically thin arms through the canvas shroud and, by virtue of an impossibly small opening, extract three or four towels.

What he did with all these towels was unclear. He may have used them simply to protect the handsome pinstriped pajamas that he wore each day, and of which he seemed to have an endless supply.

Elsewhere on the hallway came other sounds. At the far end, a woman was singing a what sounded like an old spiritual hymn while an aide hummed what might have been a Creole tune. Behind these two musical renditions was the sound of a baseball game in progress. I couldn't tell who was winning or even who was playing but could only hear the steady drone of the announcer's voice over the undulating drone of the crowd.

One reliable contributor to the hallway cacophony is my next-door neighbor, an elderly woman who resembles a dyspeptic Albert Einstein. Beyond her along the hallway is a seemingly gentle woman who usually stays in her room all day and speaks only in a foreign tongue, perhaps Italian or Portuguese.

For reasons I still fail to understand, Albert Einstein seems to despise this silent woman next door. Occasionally she bursts into long streams of profanity, mostly at night when both are in the hallway anticipating the arrival of the dinner trays.

The lady who was singling the spirituals is a former social worker with a mouth full of broken teeth. She walks up and down our corridor tap-tapping away with her cane, which she seems not to need for locomotion but for sound only.

Another regular member of our hallway contingent is a lady at the far end of the corridor who pushes a wheelchair back and forth that carries only her purse. The purpose of the wheelchair, I am told, is simply to keep her from stumbling. She looks angry or mean most times and I think of her as a superannuated Marley's Ghost.

These two women, together with regular visitors, other residents, nurses, aides, doctors, social workers and a host of others make the regular procession up and down our hallway. The aides have taken to wearing bandanas around their noses and mouths to protect them from the Covid-19 virus, making them look like outlaws about to rob a bank in an old Western.

The noise level when this circus gets into full swing can shift from the quiet of an empty church to the hellish clamor of a Victorian madhouse faster than you might expect.

# THE FIRST AND ONLY TIME

On December 21, 1988, a Pan Am Boeing 747 named *Clipper Maid of the Seas* took off from London, en route to New York. Before the plane made her big swing west over the Atlantic, a bomb blew a hole in its belly over the Scottish hamlet of Lockerbie. The wreckage was spread over several miles of emerald fields where the lambing season had just begun.

With a co-author, I had proposed to do a book on the bombing of Pan Am flight 103, but things were not going well. I had had good FBI sources for many years and planned to rely on them for help in unraveling the story of Pan Am 103 and presenting it in the pages of a book. My co-author, however, apparently had other ideas. He had long been beholden to Israeli sources and seemed be inclined to blame any act of terrorism anywhere on the world on the Palestinians. This, it turned out, was his answer to the bombing of Pan Am 103.

But that is not what happened.

I soon wound up traveling to Scotland and interviewing the local Scottish police chief, a kind and thoughtful man named John Boyd. He had been doing some minor repair work in his kitchen when the plane exploded over Lockerbie. He threw on some clothes and rushed to the scene. Between Mr. Boyd and my FBI sources, I had what I thought was a good handle on what was at that point the most significant terror investigation in U.S. history.

When I returned from Scotland, I began putting the story together as best I could, but I was lacking many of the details I would need to make a compelling narrative of book-length. I waited and waited for my co-author to provide some information from his sources, whoever they were, but he seemed to be unable to do so in a timely manner. Intensely irritated, I began writing what I knew and waited for him to provide details of his reporting.

After we delivered the book, *The New York Times* ran excerpts in its Sunday magazine, placing the story on the cover with a photograph of the cockpit of the

*Clipper Maid of the Seas* lying in one of those brilliant green fields. The headline of the story on the magazine's cover read: "Pan Am Flight 103, the German Connection." But there was no German connection. The bomb that had blown up the *Clipper Maid of the Seas* had not been made by Palestinians, as it turned out, but by a Libyan bomb maker.

Perhaps whoever made the bomb had gotten too cute. It had been rigged to two triggers: one connected to an altimeter which would trigger the bomb to go off at a certain altitude, the other rigged to a conventional timer. Somehow, the cleverly wired bomb did not go off over the Atlantic Ocean, as the bomb maker must have intended, but over little Lockerbie, Scotland. That would give investigators the opportunity to recover tens of thousands of pieces of evidence and put together a prosecution that would later bounce from Scottish courts to U.S. courts to even a Libyan court.

Wherever the evidence went, it yielded the same conclusion: Pan Am 103 had been blown up by Libyan terrorists or terrorists working for the Libyan government — not Palestinians, as my co-author and I had claimed. While writing, I was anxious because this was my first book, and I did not want to miss the deadline. Selfishly, I knew I also wanted to have a rollicking good narrative to sustain the book and make it a compelling read, but that was no excuse for what I wound up doing, which was writing something for the first and only time in my career as a journalist that I knew was false and then putting my name to it.

An enterprising man who was somewhat older than my co-author and me called us after reading the piece in the *New York Times Magazine.* He said our book would make a great movie, and he wished one of us would accompany him to Hollywood. My co-author went to Hollywood with him and they made the rounds of movie studios, but never seemed to manage to talk about the book.

My co-author finally found it his turn to become nervous and asked the man, "When are we going to talk about the book, and what are we going to say?"

The enterprising man gave my co-author a meaningful look and said, "When I bullshit, you bullshit."

When my co-author told me the story, I was sick at heart because I knew that they were not the only ones bullshitting. I, too, had been bullshitting in writing

the book as I had.

I know the rules of journalism and I violated one of the most important by allowing my name to be used on a piece of reporting that I had reason to believe was untrue.

To the families of all those who perished aboard the doomed Pan Am flight I offer my deepest and most sincere apologies.

# ELUCIDATING RUMSFELD

'Twas as tight and tidy as a hobbit's burrow—plus the place had a killer view. Lake Michigan was right below us, and you could look clear across to Chicago. Inside, however, was another story.

My wife and I had begun spending parts of our summers in Michigan each year, and this summer was no exception. But when we got there the place, despite the great view, was a dump. We had our niece with us and didn't want to subject her to this crummy place, so we quickly checked into alternative houses to rent.

The realtor who had handled the initial rental for us soon offered another. The new place belonged to a man in Chicago, she said, a man named Rumsfeld.

I couldn't believe it. I knew that Defense Secretary Donald Rumsfeld lived in Chicago during much of the year, but I hadn't thought he might have a vacation or weekend place across the lake in Michigan. He did, though, and now his house was ours, at least for two weeks.

We carried our bags and beach stuff inside, and soon made ourselves at home. The place was hardly ostentatious, a simple and functional ranch-style layout with no fuss or flair, all on one floor. Just like Rummy himself, I thought.

We explored our new environment. In the basement we found a host of exotic saws and woodworking equipment, as well as stacks of woodworking magazines that Rumsfeld had clearly subscribed to for some time.

The den was the most interesting room. There, Rumsfeld had his personal desk and on the blotter beneath the heavy glass there was a short list of phone numbers—two for Richard Nixon, one for Henry Kissinger, one for the renowned Bohemian Grove club near San Francisco, where eminent Republicans supposedly get their jollies running around in the woods naked. There were other names and numbers, but those are the only ones I remember.

What was striking about the house was its surprisingly antiseptic nature. James Mattis, a career Marine officer who would succeed Rumsfeld as Defense Secretary, was known to have a personal library of some seven thousand books. Granted, this was Rumsfeld's weekend or vacation place, and no one would expect him to keep a large library here, but there was nothing, absolutely nothing—no tomes on military history, no philosophical treatises, nothing one might have expected given Rumsfeld's public ad hoc excursions into abstruse realms of philosophy, cosmology and what have you.

For a man described as the principal architect of President George W. Bush's foreign and military policies, Rumsfeld had an astonishingly small collection of printed material that might have given some insight into the way his mind worked.

Senior officials in the Bush administration all the way up to National Security Advisor Condoleezza Rice, and even President Bush himself, made it clear that Rummy was the man with his hands on the levers of policy when it came to so-called enhanced interrogation, rendition of terrorist suspects to foreign countries, and virtually everything to do with the Iraq and Afghanistan wars, including the decisions to emphasize adherence to the warlords in Afghanistan and to conduct the notorious prison interrogations in Iraq.

Neither Iraq nor Afghanistan offered what might be called a classic military confrontation in terms Clausewitz might have appreciated, but Rumsfeld was intent on freelancing even when freelancing seemed uncalled for. Every effort to corral him on facts and figures was doomed to defeat. Often, he would rebut questions or criticisms with his trademark sarcasm, so much so that in one instance when former CIA Director John Brennan was offering a view on a subject in the Situation Room, Rumsfeld dismissed him with acid sarcasm and would not relent until the president ordered him to do so.

There were no clues in the house as to where the sarcasm might have come from. Perhaps Rumsfeld's most famous philosophic formulation derived from the basic epistemological question of, what do we know? There are, he enlightened us, known knowns, known unknowns and unknown unknowns, and the question for policymakers like himself was how to use the known to elucidate the unknown.

"Elucidate" is a word Rumsfeld might have used himself to explain the proposition. The word just happened to pop into my mind, something I imagine did not happen to Donald Rumsfeld himself all that often.

# OCCUPYING LIBERTY

U.S. officials charged with ensuring America's security often find they must sacrifice aspects of her liberty.

Striking this delicate balance on a day-to-day basis is not easy. Benjamin Franklin once said, "Those who would give up essential liberty, to purchase a little temporary safety, deserve neither liberty nor safety."

The sage of Philadelphia was a staunch absolutist on liberty, as are millions of Americans. In his important and insightful memoir, former CIA Director General Michael V. Hayden writes: "The U.S. intelligence community occupies only that portion of liberty allotted to it by the American people."

This is a foundational truth, worthy of repetition not only to the men and women who work for America's intelligence services but also to the scores of writers, reporters and editors charged with understanding and explaining U.S. intelligence work to their fellow citizens.

In my time as an editor and writer on intelligence issues for *U.S. News & World Report* and *The Washington Post*, I often found myself struggling with policy issues that made simple explanations difficult. The dark side of intelligence, which can involve assassinations, torture and kidnapping, is not always easy to explain in simple terms. Yet in all those years, I never met a single journalist who took these issues lightly or who would willingly put his nation's security at risk simply to score a journalistic coup.

But this has to work both ways. If intelligence officials want the American people to trust them to occupy a portion of their liberty in the name of national security, then they have to come out of their defensive crouches and engage with the members of the press.

If they do, they might find that we journalists are not a grudge-holding bunch of burnouts bent on taking a torch to the U.S. Constitution and Bill of Rights on a lark.

Journalists who cover intelligence take their jobs with the utmost seriousness. We respect the people we write about and would appreciate the same professional curtesy.

The beneficiaries of such an entente would, of course, be the American people.

# THE NEW NORMAL

## JANUARY 10, 2021

The other day I received my first shot of the new Covid-19 vaccine, one of about 700,000 people living in long-term care facilities that were put at the head of the line just after healthcare workers. The second jab comes in a few weeks.

You would think that receiving a life-saving vaccine in the midst of a pandemic that has already claimed 370,000 lives in this country would be a game-changing event. But alas, the infection rate and deaths from the illness continue to soar while most Americans still have months to wait before they can get their own jab.

In this place, the vaccine for many residents was just another unwanted medical intervention.

The woman who lives in the room next to mine could be heard shouting "Get away from me! Get away from me!" when the nurses came to give her the vaccination.

Down the hall is a man wrapped in bandages who reminds me of "the soldier in white" from Joseph Heller's *Catch-22*: "The soldier in white was constructed entirely of gauze, plaster and a thermometer, and the thermometer was merely an adornment left balanced in the empty dark hole in the bandages over his mouth."

The only difference between Heller's character and this guy was that Heller's soldier in white was completely silent while our man moans from morning until night. When they came to give him his Covid shot, he let out a howl that could probably be heard three blocks away.

As you may have surmised, our soldier in white elicits little sympathy on our floor because, frankly, he never shuts up. The moaning, yelling and screeching starts in the morning and carries on at various decibel levels throughout the day.

One day when the screeching was particularly bad, my friend Art, who is another long-term resident here, shouted down the hallway.

"So cut the other one off already!"

After which our soldier in white became known to the cognoscenti on our floor as "Hopalong."

"Hopalong is at it again," Art will say to me as he passes my door in the morning in his wheelchair, nodding in the direction of the infernal racket coming from down the hallway.

As you can see, the miracle vaccine, while welcome, has not really changed things that much in my little corner of the medical establishment. Every day remains a challenge. The risk of dying from Covid-19 may be less because of the new wonder drug, but the risk of dying from a thousand other things — including boredom — remains the same.

The nurse who came to give me my jab said something about how we all have to get used to the "New Normal." It's funny, but to me the New Normal seems very similar to the Old Normal.

# A TIP FROM BOB WOODWARD

When Bob Woodward walked up to my desk in *The Washington Post* newsroom, it was something of a surprise. Woodward is the world's most famous journalist and a visit to an ordinary reporter in the newsroom is something of an event.

Woodward had come on a mission. Unbeknownst to me, he had gone to the *Post's* executive editor, Len Downie, and told him of his predicament. He had received one of his amazing tips. One never knew where Bob's tips came from, and I didn't ask the provenance of this one. But it was a doozy.

The Chinese government, he had learned, had funneled an undisclosed amount of money into the Clinton-Gore reelection campaign. It was a fantastic tip, but Bob couldn't confirm it. He talked to Downie, who said, "Go see that new guy Duffy, I hear he has some great sources."

I had been at the *Post* for less than a month and I did, in fact, have some amazing sources, many of them at the top of the Federal Bureau of Investigation. I had to decide which of these sources I would pass the tip on to. I called the deputy director of the FBI, who was a friend of a good friend of mine, with whom I had written a book.

I related Bob's tip without saying it had come to Woodward. I said that we had a tip – "we" meaning the *Post*—and then relayed the substance of Bob's information about the money from the Chinese government going into the Clinton-Gore campaign.

To my surprise and delight the man invited me to meet him for coffee the next day, very early in the morning. (G-men get up early, I learned.) I did so and over coffee relayed my tip. The man seemed interested and engaged.

The Chinese *had* put money in the Clinton-Gore reelection campaign, the man told me. In fact, it had not been just some money but $3.6 million. The FBI had learned of this through a wiretap they had placed with court authorization at the Chinese embassy on Connecticut Avenue.

Wow, I thought, not only did I get the amount confirmed but I found out how the FBI had learned about it — a sources and methods question that I would never be able to address in the newspaper.

But it was a humdinger. I went back to the newsroom and walked into the office that Bob was borrowing at the time, where he'd hung his suit coat and kept his files. I sat down at the computer he regularly used and began typing. I tried to type out a lede—the first sentence of a news story—that I thought Bob would have written.

As I wrote the story I typed in our bylines: by Bob Woodward and Brian Duffy. The *Post* computer system automatically spits out the words *Washington Post Staff Writer* when you type in your name.

Bob came in several hours later and I told him that I had gotten confirmation on his tip. He was delighted. "OK," he said, "now we have to go and see Len."

Downie had a difficult job, running a newsroom with more than a hundred reporters and editors. In the internet age, trying to make sure all of them were updating their stories for the website was no easy task. He was standing behind his desk in one of the glassed-in offices along the north wall of the newsroom. Going into an editor's office there was called "going to the north wall."

We walked in, Bob and I, and Downie was immediately effusive, congratulating me on getting confirmation of Bob's tip. "But there is just one thing, Brian," Downie said. "I have to know who the source was." He must have seen a look of hesitancy on my face because he added immediately: "I don't need the name. I just need to know where he works and what he does."

I quickly relaxed and told them that the source was the deputy director of the FBI. Bob was sitting on a couch, and he gave me a funny look.

"Wow, the deputy director of the FBI. That's a pretty good source."

Only later would I learn that during Watergate, Bob's famous "Deep Throat" source had also been the deputy director of the FBI, a man named Mark Felt.

The story, with the bylines of Bob first and me second, was stripped across the *Post's* front page the next morning. It was, to me at least, like a thermonuclear device had gone off over the capitol.

People were amazed and surprised. Trying to find out who had put so much

money into the Clinton-Gore campaign had been the favorite parlor game in Washington for weeks and now the *Post* had the story and seemingly had it locked down.

The story ran that way in the first edition only. Sometime after that, Bob got the order of the bylines changed so that in all subsequent editions the story ran as follows:

*By Brian Duffy and Bob Woodward, Washington Post Staff Writers*

# CODENAME MEGA

Soon after I wrote the story with Bob Woodward, the foreign editor of the *Post,* Eugene Robinson, walked over to my desk in the newsroom. I was so new to the paper that I didn't have an office yet. But I was the investigations editor, so I guess I was the logical place to start.

Eugene told me that Nora Boustany, one of his reporters who covered the diplomatic community, had a tip about an Israeli spy working in Washington. Could I help confirm it?

This was right up my alley. As a reporter I had covered the intelligence community, both the FBI and the CIA, and had good contacts in both agencies.

This would be a question for the Bureau, I knew.

Nora was a quiet woman but with a decided instinct for the jugular when it came to reporting. We went together to interview the source, a diplomat who lived in an elegant penthouse apartment in downtown Washington. After some polite chatting we got down to cases and the diplomat said, yes, he had heard a story about an Israeli spy operating in Washington under the codename Mega. Unfortunately, he knew nothing more than that.

It wasn't much to go on but at least it was a place to start.

I had a good contact in the Bureau who oversaw Division Five, the counter-intelligence division, which ran all espionage investigations. The man agreed to speak to us, and when we met I told him what we knew: a tip had come into *The Washington Post* about an Israeli spy in Washington, probably working under diplomatic cover, who was using the codename Mega. Could he confirm the story?

The man was not a friend, as was the case with some of my other contacts in the Bureau, but he reluctantly did so.

Yes, he said, there was an investigation of an Israeli spy that the Bureau was working on, but it was still active and he could not discuss it in any detail.

That was enough for me. I asked if there was anything I needed to be aware

of, such as undercover informants or anyone who might be placed at risk if we published the story. The FBI man said there was not.

Back in the newsroom, Nora and I put the story together. We knew it was not that unusual for an ally like Israel to have agents spying on the U.S. The United States was the single biggest source of economic and military aid to the Jewish state, contributing some $3 billion a year. Safeguarding that revenue was the principal task of the Israeli diplomatic and intelligence operatives in the nation's capital.

Thus, the employment of Mega was as natural as a homeowner keeping watch on his more affluent next-door neighbor in the hope that the money lavished on the lawn and garden would keep his own property green as well. But spying by allies on each other remains a prickly subject and is usually kept tightly under wraps in the diplomatic world.

In any event, Nora and I wrote the story on deadline, and it ran on the front page of the *Post* the next day. I would not see my FBI source for many months after that, but he would tell me later that the story had caused quite an explosion in the diplomatic community. Not everyone in that community, evidently, was as comfortable with the relationship between the United States and Israel as my FBI contact was.

Mega's identity was not revealed, but the predictable political backlash ensued with congressional hearings into the matter and the powerful American Israel Public Affairs Committee, AIPAC, doing its best to keep a lid on things.

No damage to the U.S.-Israel relationship was done but the facts had been put out there for Congress and the public to make of them what they would. That, I suppose, is the best journalists can do on such a sensitive issue: get the facts out there, inform the world what's happening and let people make whatever judgements they deem proper and appropriate.

That, I believe, is how the system should work and it worked very well in that case.

But I would still like to know who Mega was.

# TWO TYPES OF JOURNALISTS?

In his brilliant biography of former Secretary of State Henry Kissinger, Walter Isaacson makes a distinction between two types of journalists: access journalists, who do day-to-day coverage, and investigative journalists. These are reporters like Seymour Hersh of *The New York Times,* who has broken many big stories, including one about how Kissinger wiretapped several former aides and reporters illegally.

As someone who has been something of a hardy perennial in the weedy garden of investigative journalism, I can say truthfully that this is a distinction without a difference.

As an investigative journalist for *U.S. News & World Report*, *The Wall Street Journal* and *The Washington Post*, I found that having access to precincts of power in agencies like the CIA and the FBI was more important than any other attribute I might bring to my professional game.

Such access is not earned easily or cheaply. Over the years I took care to cultivate senior officials who might be able to help with difficult stories on deadline. This involved daily or weekly telephone contact, frequent visits or lunches and often short notes of thanks or appreciation.

In one instance, I cultivated a senior CIA official assiduously by meeting him every other week for lunch at an expensive Italian restaurant on Dupont Circle. Over pasta and prosciutto my friend and I would talk about the news, the weather, or any errant gossip we may have heard that was simply amusing. I made a point of never asking a serious question while we were eating, but when I needed help on a story I knew I could call him.

I hope that my previous two chapters, about a Chinese government campaign contribution and an Israeli spy, show that contrary to what Mr. Isaacson claims, reporters do not need to be classified as either "access" or "investigative." The skills required apply to all journalists.

The bottom line for any reporter is trust. Without trust, no reporter, no matter their area of alleged expertise, can ever hope to extract sensitive information from a source who is sticking his neck out to provide it.

# BYE BYE BABY DOC
## 1986

It is the biggest slum in the biggest city in the poorest nation in the Western Hemisphere. Its name is Cité Soleil. The name is more than apt because the sun here is an unforgiving oven that bakes the financially crippled that must call it home because they have no other place to go.

I went to Haiti in 1986 to cover the removal from power of Jean-Claude "Baby Doc" Duvalier. Baby Doc was the son of the infamous Francois "Papa Doc" Duvalier, Haiti's self-proclaimed dictator for life.

His departure from the presidential palace in downtown Port-au-Prince would not be without event, however. A firebrand young priest named Jean-Bertrand Aristide had mobilized the legions of Haiti's poor to prevent Baby Doc from leaving with the lion's share of his country's treasury.

In the event, the young priest was not successful. When I got to the Port-au-Prince airport in the middle of the night to see the dictator off, he was met there by a large open truck stuffed to overflowing with Gucci luggage and bric-a-brac that he had stolen from the presidential palace and the other residences he maintained in and around the Haitian capital.

Washington had tried to arrange transport for the dictator to a distant country, possibly France. Things had gotten so bad that even Washington realized that Baby Doc's time had come to an end.

The struggles that tumbled through the narrow streets and alleys of Port-au-Prince were horrific. Baby Doc's soldiers fired live ammunition into the crowd, often at point-blank range, and the people responded with machetes. The picture was not pretty. The machetes were normally used to cut the sugar cane that once covered the island of Hispaniola, which Haiti shares with the Dominican Republic.

After weeks of covering this fighting most of us western reporters were at a loss to say who was winning. Every night we would repair to the hills of

Pétion-Ville, the wealthy suburb above the teeming streets and slums of Port-au-Prince. There the expensive French restaurants served meals that cost what the average family of four in Haiti could live on for a year.

This was nothing short of obscene — covering the filth and degradation of the Haitian people by day and dining by candlelight at night. A constant source of debate among us reporters was the daily body count. One night, a reporter from a big Midwestern daily arrived at one of the nicest restaurants and pronounced that that day's body count had exceeded 100. This was a first even by the standards of Haitian violence.

I was in Haiti with a friend and colleague, a young man named Yves, whose family happened to be from Pétion-Ville. Over some kind of seafood dish that cost an ungodly sum, I mentioned to Yves that this figure had to be wrong.

He nodded in agreement and said, "Let's go find out."

We knew that the morgue in downtown Port-au-Prince was only lightly guarded. Why not just go there and count the bodies for ourselves? Without saying a word to anyone, Yves and I piled into our tiny rental car and headed back down the hill toward Port-au-Prince. The streets were shrouded in darkness, but we knew the way to the morgue and went there directly.

A solitary security guard was all that stood between Yves and me and the bodies inside. While Yves distracted the guard, I pulled a piece of metal sheeting off a barred window. I yanked the metal back far enough to squeeze my arm inside the bar and opened the window. A simple hand crank opened the jalousie window. I turned it and soon Yves and I were inside.

Now came the tricky part. There were bodies everywhere, but we figured that by adding up the ones with obvious machete wounds and those with gunshot wounds we would come up with a roughly accurate reckoning of the death count. The numbers were clear: there were many more Haitians killed by machetes than by bullets. If our numbers were accurate, Baby Doc's soldiers and his Tonton Macoutes were losing and losing badly to the Haitian people.

This should have come as no news to Baby Doc or to anyone who knew Haiti's history. This was the same country, after all, that had sponsored the first slave revolt in the Western Hemisphere many decades before the American Civil War.

One thing that constantly amazed me about my time in Haiti was the sheer grit and goodness of the Haitian people. Somehow on Sunday mornings the people of Cité Soleil would rise and walk out of their slums up to the Cathedral in the central square of Port-au-Prince. Though they lived with open sewers and no running water these people were invariable clean and well dressed. They also sang like angels.

I don't know how they did it, but I believe the same grit and goodness that drove them to Mass each Sunday drove them to fight like tigers against Baby Doc's greed and brutality. Call it a triumph of the common man, if you will. Whatever it's called, it was — and is — impossible to forget.

# WASHINGTON'S ELDER STATESMAN

For those who live outside it, the world inside the Washington Beltway is an insular, clubby place. It is a place of tribal rituals and customs and even its own laws and regulations.

The problem with that is the laws and regulations made inside the Beltway are intended to govern many millions of people who live outside it, and who know little or nothing about it or the people who live and work there.

As in any such place, there are certain men and women who attain an exalted status by virtue of the length of time spent there, the offices they hold and the influence they wield.

These thoughts are occasioned by the passing this month of Vernon Jordan, a civil rights icon and Washington institution and counselor to several presidents, Bill Clinton and Barack Obama among them.

Mr. Jordan held many high positions in the corporate world but unlike other elder statesmen in the Washington world, he held no elective or appointive office. He was ever near the centers of power, however, and knew just how the levers worked.

Another elder statesman of Washington was Clark Clifford. Mr. Clifford, like Mr. Jordan, was an advisor to several Democratic administrations and a leading voice in the Democratic Party. Late in his career Mr. Clifford came to be involved in a messy financial scandal involving a major Washington bank that was acquired by the somewhat dubious international bank, Bank of Credit and Commerce International, or BCCI.

Mr. Clifford did not orchestrate whatever wrongdoing happened at BCCI but was merely too close to the mess. A partner of Mr. Clifford in the BCCI affair was Robert Altman, better known as the husband of Lynda Carter, who starred as Wonder Woman and became a big Democratic influence broker.

In looking into the BCCI matter, I spent a good deal of time trying to under-

stand the government's case against both Mr. Clifford and Mr. Altman. The trial was to be held in New York and I had occasion to be in Manhattan, so I ventured up to the courthouse to review the pleadings that had been filed in the case.

The government's pleadings alleged many things against the two men, many of them unproven and hard to substantiate. It was unclear who was the instigator in the alleged fraud attributed to Mr. Clifford and Mr. Altman, whether it was Mr. Altman or Mr. Clifford and who was the victim and who was the perpetrator. On returning to Washington, I wrote a story about the affair in *U.S. News & World Report*.

*U.S. News* was the third and smallest of the three national newsweeklies after *Time* and *Newsweek*. It also had acquired over the years something of a reputation for conservatism, although I am not quite sure why. I paid no heed to the labels applied to the magazine and thought that the only thing conservative about it was that we, as reporters and editors, refused to let the language of our written pieces outstrip the facts that supported them.

That's real conservatism, I thought, and was proud of it.

I was accustomed to writing such pieces as the magazine's Investigations Editor. What I was not accustomed to was having the subject of one of these pieces call me up and thank me. That is precisely what Mr. Clifford did after the piece ran. I was flummoxed. I did not expect his thanks or fully appreciate what it had taken him to make a call to a reporter, but in any case, I was grateful listening to his deep gravelly voice and his words of thanks and praise for my work.

I tried to explain that I did not expect thanks or praise and that I just reported the facts as I saw them. Mr. Clifford blew me off in a kindly, avuncular way and said, "Well, all the same Brian, thank you."

I came to wonder then and later about the role of elder statesman in the Washington insiders club. For many years, the Republican Party had been the party of Big Business, or so it claimed, yet for all the years they had spent in control over the White House and Congress, the Republican Party had very few elder statesmen to show for it.

The Democrats by contrast had several older statesmen of Mr. Jordan and Mr. Clifford's stature. Robert Strauss was another and they all conducted themselves

with dignity, rigor and integrity. None, however, got themselves in quite the jam that Mr. Clifford did with BCCI, and I was determined to try to figure out if it had been by accident or by deliberation.

The piece I wrote concluded that Mr. Clifford had been drawn into the BCCI matter, not by accident, but as an unwitting participant. The fraud charges brought against him by the government were without substance, I wrote, and the allegations would more properly have been lodged against Mr. Altman.

I was pleased with having gotten to the bottom of what was then one of the thorniest financial messes in Washington at the time. It had not taken more than a little reading of some government filings and a few conversations with people who knew or claimed to be in the know about what had happened. It was a big payoff, I thought, for a very modest investment on my part.

Still, I was happy to have made it and happy to have gotten the return I did on my investment. It was not lost upon me, however, that coming from a supposedly conservative magazine, an exoneration such as it was in the pages of *U.S. News* might have been worth a lot more to Mr. Clifford than if it had come from a liberal bastion like *The Washington Post*.

In any case, if that is called playing against type that is precisely what I was doing, without fully realizing it of course.

# TIME AND HEROES

Mary Beth and I had been watching the local team on TV for weeks and wanted to get out of our small apartment and go see the real thing. It was a sparkling spring day, perfect for a baseball game.

We got to Nationals Park between games of a doubleheader. We noticed a handsome older Black man standing a few rows in front of us on the concrete walkway between our section, the mezzanine, and the expensive field level seats. He wore pressed khaki pants, a blue dress shirt open at the neck, and commanded the rapt attention of a group of middle-aged white fans. They accorded his every utterance the greatest respect, and it was obvious they thought he was a person of consequence.

Curious, we walked down. As we got closer, I saw that the man was Frank Robinson, a boyhood hero of mine.

In 1966, Robinson hit 49 home runs for Baltimore and was MVP of the league and the World Series. He hammered 586 homers in a career that spanned five teams in twenty years. In the outfield Robinson covered ground like a gazelle. He had a gun for an arm, and no one was better on the base paths. Possibly even more impressive, later he became the first Black manager in the major leagues. Although he played in his prime hundreds of miles south of where I grew up on Long Island, I followed him almost every game, accomplishment by accomplishment, and there was never any shortage of those.

The man in front of us was obviously past his prime, but his fine, chiseled features remained, under a crown of white, close-cropped hair. As the crowd around him thinned out I stepped forward. Robinson flashed us a warm smile, but at the crucial moment I found I had nothing to say to my boyhood hero. I mumbled something stupid and then retreated as Mary Beth nudged me away from the group. Boyhood traits of shyness and awkwardness always seem to reappear at the most inopportune moments.

Robinson smiled at me again and I walked away happy. Sometimes, even after the passage of time, one's heroes retain a peculiar power, and the memories of a starstruck kid are not so easily compromised. Little boys, no matter how old they get, don't give up their heroes easily.

# A REPORT FROM BEHIND THE LINES

## APRIL 17, 2020

In the current health care crisis we hear a lot of talk — justifiably — about the workers on the front lines. We hear very little, however, about those of us *behind the lines.*

It has occurred to me that I am one such person. For some time, I have been living in a rehabilitation facility that is also a home for the aged and those with geriatric diseases like Alzheimer's. It is exactly the kind of place where a lot of the deaths from Covid-19 are occurring.

Though we are told nothing, we hear it in the rumor mill every day: there are people here who are infected and dying. Two nurses on the second floor were supposedly infected. One died and the other is said to be in intensive care. No one will say a word officially but that is what we hear.

There are said to be three types of intelligence: signals or Signit, human or Humint, and rumors or Rumint. You could say that here we are running on Rumint.

In this place, people simply disappear and when you ask what happened to so-and-so, you get a sympathetic smile but no information.

Such was the case with my friend Danny. He was a short man with a ready sense of humor and a self-deprecating wit. He usually dressed in red and could have passed for one of Santa's elves.

He is gone. But no one will say where, and if he died, when and what of.

Another is this lively fellow who looked like a wizened leprechaun who was a regular at our bingo table. Whenever we had a musical performer to entertain us, he would always demand to hear the Italian torch song "Amore."

He is gone too, and on grinds the rumor mill. From my post behind the lines, I can bear first-hand witness to the courage of those continuing to work in these pandemic-crisis conditions around me.

The staff is dressed in surgical gowns of various colors — yellow, green and orange seem to be the favored ones. They wear face guards with shields that look

like bulletproof glass and beneath them the ubiquitous surgical masks.

With all the protective gear it is impossible to know who you are speaking to. Not that it matters. When you ask a staff member how things are going you invariably hear: “Oh, not bad,” or “Things are OK.” The quiet way these folks go about their thankless jobs is a tribute to their heroism.

But that is little solace to the rest of us. With visitors and family kept away there is no way to know what is really happening. So we exist on rumors. Scraps of traded Rumint. People disappear suddenly without a word. Staff members carry on bravely but silently. That is Covid-19 behind the lines.

# TIGHT AND BRIGHT

Peter Cary, the guy with the desk in front of mine, had not come in yet. We didn't take attendance in *The Miami Herald* newsroom, but it was odd. He lived less than a block from me, only minutes from the newsroom.

Peter, who would become my best friend at the newsroom and remains a great friend to this day, finally showed up and he had a story: someone broke into his houseboat but didn't steal anything, just took a shower and changed his clothes.

That, I thought, was very odd. Maybe even odd enough for a story.

The *Herald* fancied itself something of a writer's paper. It had in-house competitions for best lede, best headline, and the best short story on the front page. We called the latter "Tight and Bright."

I thought this story of a burglar who stole nothing but took a shower and left his clothes behind was a great candidate for a "Tight and Bright" and told Peter so.

"Go ahead," he said, "call the cops, see what they say."

I followed his advice even though I didn't cover the local cop shop, as we called it. I got a detective on the phone and asked a leading question.

"Do you have a nickname for this guy?"

"Yeah. We call him the wash and wear burglar."

Bingo! Now I had my "Tight and Bright." I wrote it as such and it made the wire services and ended up running on front pages across the country proving, if any proof were needed, that everyone can use something to make their day a little brighter.

# THE MOST IMPORTANT STORY

I got the first call just after nine a.m. I was living in a small apartment on Wisconsin Avenue after my divorce and was scheduled to fly to New York that morning for a meeting, of all things, on the magazine's budget.

The caller was our new national editor, and he said a plane had struck the north tower of the World Trade Center.

Strange, I thought. Must be a little Cessna that got lost somehow. Even so, it seemed that flying into something like the World Trade Center could hardly have been an accident.

A second call came less than half an hour later. A plane had just hit the South Tower.

Now I knew there would be no going to New York. That was over; the budget could wait.

I drove down Wisconsin Avenue to the *U.S. News* offices in Georgetown. On every corner there seemed to be a soldier with an assault rifle. By the time I got to the magazine, people were buzzing about the attack. I went straight to my office and turned on the TV. Before long, dozens of people had crowded into my office—reporters, editors, photographers, photo editors, layout people, researchers, even the library staff.

Mort Zuckerman, who owned the magazine and with whom I was supposed to have had my meeting about the budget, was flying back from Europe in his private jet, and like all aircraft, his plane had been ordered to return to its departure point. So there would not only be no budget meeting, there was no way to contact him.

Putting out the magazine normally takes a full week. It involves assignment of stories, assignment of reporters and editors to stories, and the work of all the people in my office whose jobs I mentioned, and more. Stories were written, then edited, then assigned photographs and laid out, the pages hung along a wall in the

art department so the editors and writers could all see the look and sequence of stories. It wasn't a stately or orderly process, and it took time.

Now there would be no time. We would have to put the magazine out in one day, compressing the normal weekly process into twenty-four hours.

My girlfriend, with whom I lived, was taking her daughter to look at colleges somewhere down south, and she called in periodically to ask what was happening in New York. I told her as best I could, and then I had to get back to work.

Putting out the magazine in one day would prove to be not just a logistical nightmare, it would cost millions of dollars—millions of dollars we did not have. The internet had begun to seriously erode our advertising base, as it had that of all print publications. Because I could not ask my boss the owner of the magazine if I should do this or not, I had to make the decision on my own.

Damn the torpedoes, I decided.

"OK," I told the staff in my office, "this is probably the most important story any of us will ever cover in our careers. Now let's do it!"

I waited two beats, then added, "And let's not screw it up. Please."

# THANKSGIVING 2020

## NOVEMBER 26, 2020

Thanksgiving has always been one of my favorite holidays. No presents. No decorating. Just a lot of eating with maybe a little football afterwards. Easy.

I see on the TV news that millions of people are traveling today despite the warnings of government health authorities not to. Needless to say I am not traveling but I am not home either.

The place where I have been living for some time is home to many old and infirm people. I am not old but I am not well either. A stroke a few years ago took away my left side; my left arm and hand are completely useless and I walk with a pronounced limp.

Things could be worse. Some stroke victims lose their ability to speak or think clearly. That, thankfully, did not happen to me. And many of the residents here, despite advanced age and serious health problems, are also very nice people.

Not much fun though.

We are all alive, but you can't really call this living. Since the weather turned cold, I am barred from the one place in this nuthouse where I can usually find a bit of peace — a courtyard out back which in the summer is filled with flowers.

There comes a certain satisfaction in grappling with the circumstances that life thrusts upon you. It may not be much, but it's about all we've got here.

I don't think turkey and cranberry sauce is actually on the menu here today, which is fine by me. Never cared for the stuff. I will celebrate the day with a slice of pumpkin pie that my mother is bringing by. I won't see her, though, because with the Covid-19 pandemic still raging, she is not allowed in the building.

So the day will pass as all other days pass. We do the best we can. I realize that is hardly the most stirring battle cry one can imagine, but there it is.

So while others are racing through airports and driving on crowded highways, I will wish them well as I dig into my pumpkin pie.

Others tell me it's hard not to get down on days like this. But I stay vigilant against that attitude. I watch the TV news, curse the stupidity in Washington, send

texts and emails to friends and former colleagues and scribble thoughts on my blog.

I have to because the other way leads to despair, and I ain't going there.

# MORTALITY MAKES HER BED

Mortality makes her bed in the place where I live, and like a dark cloud in a delft sky or a foul-smelling fishwife she is not easily ignored.

The other night my friend from down the hall came by and asked me how he could get more therapy. This is a question about which I have great interest because I am in this place to learn how to walk again after having a stroke. I told my friend to go down to the gym on the first floor where the director of therapy has an office, and she could help get more therapy or at least he could talk to her. She is a kind, caring person who must know her business as she is a Muslim woman hired by the Jewish men who own and operate this facility. She genuinely seems to care about those of us who are here for therapy.

My friend is, like most of us here, confined to a wheelchair. He is a man of substance who was an engineer before he became ill and fell in a parking lot. He was taken by police to a hospital. His job was designing and building machines that make turbines for jet aircraft engines. He has three patents to his name, he tells me.

At the dinner hour my friend came back to my room, and I asked him how his visit with the therapy director had gone.

"Not bad," he said matter-of-factly, as if he were describing the lumps in his breakfast oatmeal or the fact that his clothes has come back from the laundry with wrinkles. "She told me my condition is untreatable. "

"That's terrible," I said.

"No," my friend said, "it's not so terrible. I'm 90 years old, my kids are doing great, my grandkids are great. I have no regrets."

"Did she tell you anything else?"

His face lit up.

"Good news. She said I could come to the gym anytime they're not busy and use the machines or work out."

# AFGHANISTAN

It has the magic and majesty and all the truth and timelessness of Tolkien. But it is a hard place, too, of cold mountains and crumbling castles – an eerie emptiness at the edge of the world.

I knew none of this before I went to Afghanistan, only that it was the place where the Cold War had come to a final crushing end. It was a place where Russia and America fought a dark and devastating war in the shadows. It had been called a proxy war, even though there had been no proxy pain or proxy blood and no, surely, proxy deaths.

I wanted to know, before I sent any of our journalists to the country, what it was like. But I also wanted to know what it was like from the perspective of the people who lived there.

Fortunately, on the *U.S. News* staff we had a photo editor who had been born in Afghanistan. I asked her if she might like to see the land of her birth. Wazhma said she would, but explained that she remembered very little of it, as she had left as a two-year-old, carried on the back of a donkey in a cradle.

If she went, Wazhma said she would have to bring her mother.

We were a most implausible traveling trio. The mother was elderly, or at least seemed so, although Wazhma could not have been more than 20 or 25 years old. Somehow, though, we soon found ourselves on a dusty street in Kabul, the Afghan capital. And almost before we knew it, we were standing in front of the house where Wazhma had lived as a child.

Over the coming days and weeks, we would retrace the steps of Wazhma and her family, a prosperous family living in Afghanistan at one of its most prosperous times. They had a king who was revered as a righteous man who ran a good government, kept the warlords mostly at bay and did his best to control the rampant opium trade.

The Soviet-Afghan war from 1979 to 1989 has been called a proxy war be-

cause the Central Intelligence Agency secretly funneled billions in weapons to the Mujahideen fighters who ultimately were able to drive out the Soviet army.

There was a grim reality to almost every aspect of it. I wanted to know all about the Russians, the Americans and the Afghans who did the fighting, and the Afghan families who had lost loved ones, and ask them if it was indeed a proxy war.

During the weeks of our visit, I would come to understand more of how Afghan families lived their lives and what they fought for and believed in. Their faith was fierce and unyielding. They didn't trifle with troublemakers. This I would come to know through my travels with Wazhma and her mother.

It may not have been the most logical way of trying to understand an impossible place, but it worked for me, and I will never forget it. Afghanistan, in a very strange but very real way, still lives in my soul.

# BUZKASHI

The man standing in front of me in Kabul, Afghanistan, was one of the biggest I had ever seen, with great ham-fisted hands.

I was in Afghanistan not long after the 9/11 attacks because as editor of *U.S. News & World Report* I wanted to assess the situation before sending any of our reporters or photographers there. As a journalist visiting from the United States, I was accorded the status of minor dignitary, but this man was a true celebrity, the captain of the local buzkashi team in Kabul, the capital of Afghanistan.

Buzkashi is the national sport of Afghanistan, a beautiful but brutally violent game which is played on horseback, and it is magnificent to see the scrum of men and horseflesh storm from one end of the scarred field to the other. It is not unlike American football, the objective being to move the ball from one end of the field to the other, but instead of a ball, in buzkashi the players use the carcass of a goat. This might well explain the man's big hands, which I noticed again as I extended my own small one toward him.

In the match before the one I had come to see, I was told that one of the horses had galloped into the stands, killing seven spectators.

I would remember the moment I met this man many years later when I joined National Public Radio as managing editor for news. It was just my second day on the job, and I had a long to-do list. At the top of the list was NPR's 50 foreign news bureaus, more than any U.S. news organization except *The New York Times*. Many of those bureaus were in dicey places, but places where important news was likely to occur. That made it difficult to keep people safe and this worried me.

Of all the bureaus, none was more threatened than the one in Kabul. Every day, it seemed, there were attacks with rocket-propelled grenades, machine guns and, probably most dangerous of all, improvised explosive devices, or IED's. IED's could blow up a truck or a car or blow the leg off a soldier, or, for that matter, a visiting journalist.

I was no security specialist, but I had written a book some years before with a colleague on the first Gulf War and had made some contacts in the Pentagon. I decided to call one, a career Army officer I had gotten to know quite well. Harry had served in Lebanon during the worst of the fighting there and had also been posted to Afghanistan and other hot spots in south Asia.

I explained my concerns and the man was unperturbed. "No problem," he said. "I have a team in-country. They'll handle it."

Afghanistan is a strange and beautiful place. Flying into the international airport, one sees the wreckage of past wars. Afghanistan has long played a central role in the Great Game between superpowers and has been overrun at various times by Pakistani armies, British forces, and lastly and most infamously, the Soviet Union in 1979. The Afghan people, therefore, are no strangers to war and violence but the Taliban, with their black flag belligerence, were something new entirely.

The Taliban forbade music and placed harsh restrictions on women and their education and general role in society. The American troops that President Bush sent to Afghanistan after the 9/11 attacks had been assigned to uproot the Taliban regime, which had given shelter to Osama bin Laden. The mission, however, would come to be much greater than that. It would eventually turn into America's longest war, lasting more than two decades, and become something of a mission to effect regime change, replacing the Taliban with a democratically elected government that the Afghan people seemed neither to want nor to understand.

It was into this situation that I came as a young reporter, trying to make sense of the chaos while ensuring the security of our own reporters and native Afghans on our staff. Of all the many environments I had encountered as a journalist, none was so foreign and full of fearsome prospects as Afghanistan. The special forces operators I had contacted while at NPR were as good as their word and helped restore security to the Kabul news bureau so that our journalists could continue to conduct interviews and carry out the duties of reporters and editors everywhere. It was a start, but I could see that the task was far larger than I had imagined.

# WHEN THE BLOOM IS REALLY OFF THE ROSE

## DECEMBER 6, 2020

In the place where I live there is a man down the hall who has Parkinson's Disease. He is confined to a wheelchair, his hands tremble and he is 91, which he is at pains to tell everyone.

On my right is a wizened old woman who looks innocent but is not to be trifled with. The other morning the two met outside my door.

The two nonagenarians circled each other like a couple of feral cats.

"When did your daughter visit you last?" the woman said to the Parkinson's man in a somewhat scolding tone. Visits by children are a point of pride in this place.

The man mumbled something I didn't quite catch but the look on his face suggested that he thought it might be a bit of witty repartee. Then he said quite clearly: "What are you doing tonight?"

The wizened woman requires a walker to stand erect. At this comment she grasped the walker and stood a bit straighter and taller.

And in a voice loud enough to be heard at the other end of the hallway she spat: "Nothing with you!"

Many mornings the Parkinson's man glides his wheelchair to the laundry cart in the hallway and silently steals a bath towel, which he then wraps around his neck. This gives him something of the raffish charm of a World War II fighter pilot.

The man's charm is evidently not as great as he thought.

# SURFIN' USA

## DECEMBER 20, 2020

Somewhere in New York State Health Department rules there must be a regulation about how shiny hallways need to be in facilities like the one where I live. Here the floors are as smooth and shiny as a skating rink, and they reflect the light with such brilliance that you would think you were stepping into a penny arcade.

The observation comes to mind because many of us here who are unable to walk go about in wheelchairs propelled largely by our own feet. Alas, when the floors are polished to the lustrous brilliance of a precious stone these feet can gain no purchase and the locomotion stops.

The other day there were three such chair jockeys in the hallway, each pedaling furiously but going nowhere. If it were a cartoon, you might see little puffs of smoke coming from beneath each chair.

One man who is ambulatory walks by my room several times a day pushing a small metal cart normally used to carry containers of oxygen. The other day I was at the junction of two long hallways and saw him take a running start, then jump on the cart when it reached top speed and slide gloriously down the hallway for a good twenty feet before coming to a halt. The last few feet he put his hands out as if he were flying, à la Leo DiCaprio in *Titanic*. I gave him a clap and he gave me a thumbs-up.

It turns out there are endless opportunities for surfing along these highly polished hallways. Moments ago I saw my friend with the cart zoom past my door flashing a V for victory.

The other day another one of our residents, an old woman, was sitting motionless in her wheelchair in the hallway.

"I can't do nothing!" she suddenly cried out.

An aide walking by said: "If you can't do nothing then don't do nothing."

"But I don't want to do nothing," the woman sobbed.

# PAKISTAN

To U.S. national security officials, one nation sits at or near the top of the list of the world's problem nations. To American journalists working on national security issues, one nation sits at or near the bottom of the list of nations considered desirable destinations and known for ease of access to national security information. That nation is Pakistan.

One of only nine countries possessing nuclear weapons, Pakistan is known to export terrorism to trouble spots around the globe and to support the repressive Taliban regime in neighboring Afghanistan. Its Inter-Services Intelligence agency, or ISI, for decades cooperated with the American CIA in counterterrorism activities, but the relationship between the two agencies has been fraught, tense and characterized at times by mendacity and downright mean-spiritedness.

I went to Pakistan after 9/11 to talk with ISI officials about both their support for the Taliban and their protection of Osama bin Laden. I did not know then that bin Laden was sheltered in a walled compound some forty miles from Islamabad, the Pakistani capital, and just three miles from a Pakistani army headquarters building. The world's most hunted terrorist was living in a barred room without bodyguards, accompanied by several of his five wives and many of his two dozen children.

After bin Laden was killed by Navy Seals in a 2011 raid authorized by President Barack Obama, an elaborate cover story would be concocted and sold to the world as the final chapter of bin Laden's misbegotten life. Almost all the cover story was false.

As detailed in Seymour M. Hersh's remarkable *The Killing of Osama bin Laden*, the final hours of the master terrorist were not at all pretty. Inside the compound, bin Laden's living arrangements were shabby and sorry. The place was a wreck. Remarkably, in a land where nearly everyone owns a gun, there were no guns in the entire compound.

After the Obama administration went public with its cover story, senior officials would describe bin Laden having engaged in a firefight with the Navy Seals, who had flown hundreds of miles through Pakistani airspace to kill him. By then, bin Laden was not the feared terrorist that the world thought it knew, but an elderly and infirm man suffering from a debilitating illness of unknown origin. Senior Obama administration officials would claim that bin Laden fought a gun battle with the Seals, trained killers of high proficiency who ordinarily would have no difficulty subduing such a frail and feeble target.

The firefight could not have happened, despite the Obama team's assertion, because as Hersh points out, there were no guns to *have* a firefight. Other stunners from Hersh's book are that bin Laden was not tracked to the compound in the garrison city of Abbottabad by superior detective work or satellite surveillance. Rather, a senior ISI official simply walked into the U.S. Embassy in Islamabad one day and reported that bin Laden had been living in a compound for some months. The man was not motivated by retribution for 9/11, but by what motivates people everywhere—money. The reward for the capture or killing of bin Laden stood at twenty-five million dollars, and the walk-in, as the man was known, wanted a fat chunk of that money.

The Obama team also asserted that Pakistani officials had not been alerted to the bin Laden raid. Hersh's book, however, describes how two senior ISI had been briefed in detail about the operation, and arranged for the Navy helicopters to fly across hundreds of miles of the country without interference. The ISI was so willing to cooperate with its American partners that it had arranged for electricity to be cut off during the hours the raid was set to occur.

I do not know Seymour Hersh, but I have long been a great fan of his investigative journalism. As someone who has spent considerable time covering, or attempting to cover, agencies like the CIA and the FBI, I am in awe of Hersh's ability to find and obtain secrets that I would kill my favorite dog for.

After my divorce some years ago, I lived for a time in an apartment directly above Hersh's apartment in the Kalorama neighborhood of Washington, D.C. I met Hersh on only one occasion, a sidewalk encounter in D.C. when he was accompanied by a friend and colleague of mine. But I did not know him.

Having now read three of his books, I feel as if I know the man better, and have taken to heart one of the injunctions in his memoir. Read, Hersh enjoins journalists, before you write. No better advice has ever been given to reporters like me, I believe, and had I been able to read Hersh's book before going to Pakistan, my trip might have been much more productive and informative.

Next time, Sy, I'll do a better job, I promise.

# THE TONSORIAL TERRORIST

Some reporters battle for the smallest, least significant scraps of information, thinking their lives depend on it. Others simply stumble on single facts that somehow tell a story better than a fat dossier filled with footnotes.

The latter describes a recent piece of reporting by veteran investigative journalist, Peter Bergen. Mr. Bergen has appeared on television and in many print outlets and has published three recent books on Osama bin Laden and his al Qaeda terrorist network. Mr. Bergen is also a founder of the National Security Archive and an expert in military law enforcement and intelligence matters.

In one of his recent books, in what was almost an aside, Mr. Bergen reported that the Navy Seals who conducted the raid on bin Laden's compound in Abbottabad, Pakistan, were unsure if they had the right target because the man they killed had a markedly darker beard than that of bin Laden in recent photographs.

Mr. Bergen said that bin Laden had used Just for Men hair dye to remove much of the gray from his bushy beard. Osama bin Laden had multiple wives, the youngest of them a teenager some three decades younger than he was, and evidently looking younger became important to him.

Even cold-blooded killers and mass murderers, it seems, like to look nice for the ladies.

# A FABLE

Once upon a time there were two baby boys born to two fabulously wealthy families who lived in very different parts of the world. Because of their families' wealth they were rich themselves.

As the babies grew into manhood, despite surface differences their lives had much in common. One man lived in a country ruled by a king. The other man lived in a country where he came to think he *was* king.

One man, a Muslim, took many wives. The other man, a Christian, had only one wife (at a time, anyway) but conducted himself as if he wanted many.

One man grew up in Queens but always wanted to live in Manhattan. The other man knew nothing of Queens but would one day bomb part of Manhattan.

One man became the leader of a terrorist organization and attacked the symbols of American military and financial might. The other man became the leader of the United States and attacked the symbol of America's political might and the seat of its democracy.

One man dyed his beard. The other man dyed his hair.

Though they moved in vastly different circles, the two men were equally preoccupied with their passions and power, and neither loser lived happily ever after.

# IN THE CLEAR

They told me I was cleared the other day. The first indication of my new status was that the signs that had been put up on my door were taken down. One was an orange sign with the words "DROPLET PRECAUTIONS." Another green sign carried a similar warning and a third, a round sun on a white rectangle, somehow warned of "coughing."

Those signs kept many people out of my room, including the doctors who were scheduled to visit me from time to time.

This is the state of affairs in the age of the coronavirus in the institution where I am living, a rehabilitation center with many old and infirm residents.

A peculiarity of these medical institutions is that those of us inside — behind the lines if you will — are given absolutely no information about what is happening. A kindly doctor told me off the record that two whole floors of this four-floor institution are now devoted exclusively to coronavirus patients. But officially, those of us living in the very midst of this pandemic are told nothing at all.

The staff rush here and there at all hours dressed in their hazmat-looking suits with funny blue footwear that look like clown shoes. One staff member told me that these shoes are usually worn by patients with neuropathy in their feet.

New York Governor Andrew Cuomo said Monday that the state would take "additional steps" to protect those in nursing homes. If nursing facilities cannot provide the appropriate level of care for any reason, they must transfer the person. All nursing home staff must now be tested for COVID-19 twice a week, and hospitals cannot discharge patients to a nursing home unless they test negative for the coronavirus.

With one-third of the 80,000 U.S. coronavirus deaths now coming just from nursing home residents and staff, "additional steps" would well seem to be required. And while you're at it, Mr. Governor, how about a little Freedom of Information for those of us on the inside? I don't need some doctor or nurse or

twenty-something nurse's aide to protect me from the truth. I have a right to know what is happening.

But I will leave such soapbox haranguing for another time. For the moment I am content to enjoy my new status of "Covid-19 negative." The warning signs of DROPLET PRECAUTIONS are gone, and I no longer feel like a leper.

And — wonder of wonders — today I was able to leave my room for the first time in weeks and do my physical therapy by walking up and down the hallway.

Happy days!

# THE VOICE OF GOD

I don't remember exactly when I switched over from sports radio to listening to NPR, but my first memory of hearing an NPR newscast is etched indelibly in my mind.

The voice on my bedside radio was saying something about a military operation that had gone terribly wrong. The year was 1980, and I was in graduate school in Chicago. President Jimmy Carter had evidently authorized an overnight military operation to rescue dozens of Americans held hostage in Tehran.

The hostages had been page one news for months. Ted Koppel was airing a nightly broadcast on ABC News called "America Held Hostage." Whatever happened in the desert outside the Iranian capital was not good. But the voice on my bedside radio sounded like the voice of God and made it sound enormously important.

That voice belonged to a gentleman named Carl Kasell. Mr. Kasell, who died this week, was an unflappable professional. It didn't hurt that he actually did sound like God.

Before I went to work at NPR, I had come to be able to identify the individual correspondents and anchors by their voices alone. Mr. Kasell was in a class by himself. His rich baritone truly did sound as if it was coming from the heavens above. He enunciated each word clearly and succinctly. His voice sounded like the voice of integrity, assuring you that what he had just said you could take to the bank. He was the real deal.

I met Mr. Kasell during my first week at NPR. I could hardly believe that the voices I was hearing outside my office on the third floor of the old NPR building on Massachusetts Avenue in Washington D.C. were the same voices I had heard for all those years on my radio.

Another one of those voices who came into my office in that first week belonged to Mara Liasson. The veteran national political reporter had been one of

my favorites for years, although I am not a political person at all. A second or two after my office door flew open, Mara was standing in front of my desk demanding that I call the White House and read someone over there the riot act. Evidently, someone in the Obama White House had snubbed her or said something unforgivably stupid.

I suppose I could have pleaded that it was just my second day on the job but that would have been wimping out. Plus, Mara was one of my heroes; how could I possibly say no? So I picked up the phone and called the White House Chief of Staff's office. After introducing myself, I said, "Listen you so and so, I don't know who said what to Mara Liasson, but she is some kind of pissed and on the warpath. I would appreciate it if someone there could straighten it out." Whatever the poor soul on the other end of the line said to me I can no longer remember, but I would be surprised indeed if it were printable.

In any case, between Carl Kasell and Mara Liasson and all the other amazing professionals at NPR, I had an unforgettable education in how to be a good journalist. Be fair, play it straight and get it right. Those were the rules we all lived by. Today, when those rules may seem quaint and old fashioned, they are more needed than ever.

In this age of alternative facts and alleged fake news, thank God for journalists like Mr. Kasell and Ms. Liasson who hold our standards high. We need more of them today – a whole lot more.

# SKATING THE TRUTH

If they're handing out medals for mendacity outside the pearly gates, chances are lots of us will be lining up behind a nice old guy with steel grey eyes, a terminal case of dishevelment and a face like an unmade bed.

That would be William Casey. History has not been kind to Ronald Reagan's campaign chairman and CIA director. Possessed of a capacious memory and a mind like a supercomputer, Casey was a true polymath. A man of letters, he knew the ins and outs of high finance and the intricacies of tax law. Though most of his tax treatises were unreadable by mere mortals, there was no denying he could get to the bottom of a mess of numbers faster than a Cray supercomputer.

He was possessed of many other talents as well. A legendary mumbler, Bill Casey could skate the truth even when that was not his intention. After the Iran-Contra affair that marred Reagan's second term in office, Bob Woodward of *The Washington Post* approached Casey's hospital bed and asked him why he had shipped missiles to the ayatollahs in Iran and paid for them with weapon sales to the Contra rebels in Nicaragua. According to the *Post*, Mr. Casey replied, "Because I believe." According to Mr. Casey's biographer, what he really told the Mr. Woodward was, "Please leave." That was the famous Casey mumble at work.

But Mr. Casey could shade the truth when the chips were down, that's for sure. After Mr. Reagan asked Mr. Casey to assume the leadership of the CIA, such was the concern about Mr. Casey's relationship with the truth and his ability to convey it, Mr. Reagan asked storied naval admiral and National Security Agency executive Bobby Ray Inman to become Mr. Casey's deputy.

Not long after I became the intelligence beat reporter for *U.S. News & World Report*, Foreign Editor John Walcott suggested that I "make the pilgrimage" to Austin, Texas to meet with Admiral Inman. Walcott had covered the intelligence beat himself with distinction for *The Wall Street Journal* and he was my boss, so I didn't have much choice. Plus, Inman was a legend in the American intelligence community, so I gladly made the trip.

In Austin, Inman told me a story that I had heard once before, about his first trip to Capitol Hill with Casey. Casey and Inman had an appointment to meet with Senator David Boren, chairman of the Senate Select Committee on Intelligence, one of two key Hill committees that provides the agency's budget. Keeping the senators happy is a large part of a CIA executive's job.

Dave Boren was one of the true gentlemen of the Senate. A former governor of Oklahoma who would go on to become the respected President of the University of Oklahoma, Boren was not a man who trifled with the truth. After a brief round of introductions, the senator pulled Admiral Inman aside out of Mr. Casey's hearing.

"Admiral," Senator Boren said, "let me tell you something. When you come up here to testify with Director Casey before me and my committee, any time you know that he is lying, I expect you to lean down under the witness table and pull up your socks."

Senator Boren had told me the same exact story so when I got back to Washington I naturally put it in the magazine. A week later, Inman called me and was none too pleased. Our conversation in Austin, he reminded me, had been on background and not for publication.

Because I had the same story from Senator Boren, I thought I should be able to use it. Not so, I realized. I had not satisfied the technical requirements of the journalist's two-source rule since my conversation with Inman had not been for the record.

Inman was right to have called me on having violated the background rule and I was wrong to have done so. Learning a new beat sometimes is all about learning from your mistakes, but that was a stupid and painful one I should not have made. It's a lesson I have not forgotten and will never forget. Journalism is about being fair, and I had violated the most important rule – the fairness rule.

# GEORGE

The lights go on every day at 5 a.m. sharp. George was always up well before that, and if he added a “please” to his daily plea for help, you knew it was going to be a bad day.

George was one of the older people in the nursing home where I live, and he managed to annoy nearly everyone by playing his television at full blast because he was stone deaf. His neighbor from across the hall used to sneak into his room and turn down the TV when George wasn’t paying attention, which was much of the time because he was 96 and had to sleep often.

Yesterday George died, so we will no longer be hearing the daily bellow for help from our crusty, curmudgeonly friend and neighbor. Death is not an infrequent visitor to nursing homes, because most people who live in them are old and sick. Nevertheless, I will miss George’s daily bellow for help and his alert to the rest of us about whether there were enough aides working that day to provide the rest of us with help. May he rest in peace; flights of angels see thee to thy rest, George.

# THREE PATENTS FOR COVID

## FEBRUARY 10, 2022

My neighbor was a 91-year-old aerospace engineer with three patents, who had a wasting disease that prevented him from standing, which always got him in trouble with the nurses' aides when he asked to be taken to the bathroom.

Then he got Covid.

When they came to take him to the Covid floor yesterday, he cried.

I will miss him. He was a good guy.

# TRAVELING FOR A STORY

One great thing about being a journalist is that you get to travel. One bad thing is you often travel to places almost no one else wants to go to, places like war zones, weapons depots and weather-ravaged cities and states. And when you get to these garden spots, very often it is impossible to see and talk to the people most worth seeing and talking to.

This was not the case with a trip I was privileged to take with a group of top government officials and journalists to Israel and Saudi Arabia. I was the editor of *U.S. News & World Report* at the time, and the owner of the magazine, Mortimer B. Zuckerman, had been scheduled to go on the trip. But at the last minute, Mort had to cancel, and I was invited in his stead by the organizer, Martin S. Indyk, a former U.S. ambassador to Israel and special envoy to the Middle East who would later become Assistant Secretary of State for Near East Affairs. It didn't hurt that Martin was also my next-door neighbor.

We arrived in Jerusalem on the night the aerial bombardment of the first Gulf War began. I had a contract to write a book on the war, and this backdrop to our trip was as exciting as it was unnerving.

Martin had arranged for us to have dinner with General Avihu Ben-Nun, commander of the Israeli Air Force, a decorated combat pilot who had been promoted out of the cockpit and up the chain of command. Over dinner, the general gave me one of those details on which great reportage is so often based. He told me that the Israeli Air Force had secretly secured overflight rights from the government of Jordan, that allowed Israeli jets to patrol Jordanian air space to prevent Iraqi aircraft incursions into Jordan and toward the Israeli border.

It was not the stuff of screaming headlines, but a nice detail I could include in the book, and I was delighted to have it. This was in the days before cell phones, so the only way I could get the information back to my co-author was by faxing it to Washington, which I did, citing the general by name but saying we needed to

keep his identity secret.

The next stop was Saudi Arabia. Riyadh, I am reliably told, is properly translated as "The Gardens," though a first-time visitor to the desert capital of the Saudi kingdom might wonder what became of all the lush garden greenery. These days, sleek superhighways slice between soaring skyscrapers, from the upper floors of which modern Saudi businessman may still see burnoose-clad Bedouins trekking their tired camels across the burning sand, in timeless tribute to ancient desert caravans.

Among our travel party was a razor-sharp young Saudi named Adel Al-Jubeir, at the time a junior official in the Saudi embassy in Washington, who years later would become the Saudi ambassador to the United States and remain a good source for me and many American journalists. Adel introduced us to Saudi royals whom few visitors to the country get to see. Thanks to Adel, we met the princes who ran the Saudi intelligence and security ministries. But Saudis, it seems, especially royals, don't like talking about the rough neighborhood they live in. They especially dislike talking about Iran, the theocratic autocracy next door that represents the Shia branch of Islam, while the Saudis are mostly Sunnis.

Our hosts entertained us in fabulous palaces, with plush furniture in vast rooms, where courtiers in long, flowing robes sat in gilt-edged chairs lining the walls. The princes, of course, sat in places of honor, and we were gathered before them like obedient students before a strict master. We had been told not to expect anything like forthright conversation during our visit, and we were not disappointed. The Saudis were obviously concerned with Iraq's invasion of Kuwait because it threatened their country and its vast oil reserves, but not once during our week-long stay was the word "Iran" mentioned, or its government discussed. We thus left Riyadh, city of gardens past but not present, unenlightened as to the inner workings of the kingdom, its citizens, and its relations with the other countries in their rough neighborhood.

Back in Israel we stayed in The American Colony Hotel in East Jerusalem, a fabulous place full of history where many a movie star, statesman and power broker has signed the guest registry over the years. Who knows how the likes of us made it through the doors, but assuredly Martin's influence had plenty to do with

it. He had contacts seemingly everywhere, and he never failed to arrange for us to have inside access to top government officials wherever we went.

By the time we got back to Washington, I had a far better understanding of the foreign policy implications of the Iraq War than before we made the trip. That's what good travel can do for a journalist, and I was delighted to have been asked to come along on this journey. I made contacts as a reporter that I use to this day, and I can't thank my friend and neighbor Martin enough. The trip was an enormous privilege, and so different from others I made as a reporter that it stands in a class by itself in my memory.

# JOURNALISM AND PUBLIC SERVICE

The reporter came to me with what I thought was an impossible proposition, but an important one. Joseph Shapiro had been examining the nation's special education classrooms as part of his beat covering social services for *U.S. News & World Report*.

I was the magazine's investigations editor. There were, Shapiro told me, too many minority kids in special ed classes. I groaned inwardly. How many environmental and economic factors conspired to produce such a situation? And how would you untangle them from mental health and other factors? It was a daunting proposition.

Journalism, at its highest level, must address grave threats to the public interest. What could be more in the public interest than helping disabled kids overcome their disabilities?

The reporter was good, but soft-hearted, and some of our unkinder colleagues said, probably soft-headed too. But he would go on to write a penetrating, prize-winning book on disabled Americans called *No Pity: People with Disabilities Forging a New Civil Rights Movement*. It addressed the Americans with Disabilities Act passed by Congress in 1990.

If we were going to make the case that Shapiro put to me, and make it in a clear and compelling way, we would have to back it up not just with anecdotal information but with facts and statistics. We would have to visit special education classes, interview kids and teachers, understand the curriculum and understand the teaching techniques being used.

Then we would have to address the numbers. This was where I knew it would get tricky. A year before I had read a Pulitzer Prize-winning series in the *Atlanta Journal-Constitution* newspaper on redlining, or discrimination by banks and insurance companies against people who live in poor neighborhoods. The series was great but reading the stories was not easy. They were dense with data and arcane descriptions of banking regulations and insurance requirements. The stories were aimed not so much at the general public, but at policy makers who could force the situation to change.

If our series were to be successful, we would have to build the stories in much the same way and the case would have to be airtight.

This, after much work by a team of reporters, we were somehow able to do. When we completed our reporting, we took the stories and our statistical findings to then Education Secretary Richard Riley.

Riley was a kind and courtly man who could have easily seen fit to throw us out of his office. But he didn't and he listened to what we had to say. What we wanted, I explained to him, was change. We wanted the rules changed. What we had found during our reporting was that Washington incentivized local school districts to put more kids into special ed classes by paying them according to the numbers enrolled in such classes. So there was a financial incentive for local school districts to derail more kids from the mainstream and shunt them off into special ed.

Instead of politely listening to our case and then dismissing us, in the manner of many Washington bureaucrats, Riley invited more people to join the discussion, particularly his advisors on special education. He had his team sit down with our team and we went through the numbers and the reporting together.

In the end, Riley said he would make rule changes and introduce legislation into the next Congress to address the problems in the special education programs that we had identified.

It was, I thought, the way journalism and public service should work. Not exactly hand in glove but at least one hand washing the other.

# PANDEMIC FRAUD

Soon after the pandemic struck, Washington began pushing billions of dollars into paralyzed businesses and into the pockets of people who had lost their jobs.

The money came with few strings attached and little in the way of oversight. Naturally, many who took the money were tempted to cheat, and cheat they did.

According to a report in *The New York Times* this past week, thousands of Americans stole billions of dollars from the federal government through pandemic aid fraud. The Justice Department is now pursuing an unprecedented 39,000 investigations into the mess.

The fraud, the largest in U.S. history, was uncovered by a technique used by investigative journalists called computer assisted reporting. It is exactly what it sounds like, using computers to help reporters dig deeper into the penetralia of massive government spending programs.

Were it not for the computers used by the *Times* reporter, David Fahrenthold, the pervasive extent of the fraud might never have been uncovered.

Human beings will always be tempted to cheat and cut corners, but today, thanks to modern technology, journalists can catch up with them.

Journalism isn't always about catching up with people and catching them out. Sometimes it is about pointing out problems, as Mr. Fahrenthold did in his report.

With luck and good sense, the government will find those who cheated and take proper precautions so it does not happen again. That, too, is what good journalism is about.

Madison and Jefferson said that a robust press corps is essential to the functioning of a robust democracy. That includes catching cheats.

Human beings are capable of great good. But, as we know, they are also capable of sliding into sloth and sinfulness. Journalists are not priests trying to make people pay for their sins. They are more accessories of good government, helping make sure the system works as it was meant to work.

# LEAKS

I knew what it was the second I saw it. The torn transcript reflected a cryptic conversation about a subject neither person wanted to discuss. I didn't know the who, the what, the where or the why; I only had to imagine the how. Clearly, the discussion was about a subject neither person wished to make clear. The obvious conclusion was that the discussion centered on something illegal or immoral, or possibly even worse.

I had good contacts in the FBI, among them several friends. I could start there. A few quick calls revealed that the conversation transcribed and given to me was the subject of a federal investigation involving illegal narcotics transactions. This meant I would have to proceed carefully and cautiously. Such investigations often involved the use of informants and sometimes even agents themselves operating within the ranks of the organized crime entity. Such people were frequently at great risk and would have to be protected. Whatever I did with this information, if anything, I would have to treat it with extreme care.

A few more calls resulted in an invitation to come over to the Hoover Building, the headquarters of the FBI. I walked into a large room expecting to see several friends but was instead surprised to see a room full of suits, mostly men I had never met before. There was an obvious tension to the group, perhaps even hostility.

One man stepped forward immediately. He was about my height but extremely fit, and wound tight as a coil.

"You Duffy?"

I said I was.

"You write anything about this," the man said, "and I'll throw your ass out that fucking window."

I had been looking out a window of the Hoover Building into a rain-slicked street below. I quickly explained that I did not plan to write anything about the

transcript I had been given, which is why I had been invited to this meeting.

The man seemed mollified, but only slightly. For as long as there has been journalism and journalists, there have probably been leaks. Jesus described the scribes and the Pharisees, but it is not known if the apostles leaked to the writers of the gospels.

Leaked information can sometimes serve a useful purpose not only for the person who receives the leak, but also for the person who authorizes the leak. In some quarters in the nation's capital, leaking has become the equivalent of an Olympic sport, with various participants leaking information so fast and furiously that it is a wonder they have time to do their regular jobs.

My position on leaks has always been to treat them with extreme care because one never knows, as with the transcript I had received of this conversation about a narcotics transaction, if someone might be at risk if the information is disclosed. In this instance, several agents of the FBI and the U.S. Drug Enforcement Administration had been working undercover against an organized crime family in New York that was involved in drug smuggling.

As a result of the way I handled the information I had been given, I was invited to New York on the occasion of the takedown of the investigation. The operations center of the FBI is in a downtown office building, and I was invited to be there the night the Bureau brought its investigation to a sudden conclusion. Arrest teams of agents had been sent out to pick up participants in the illegal scheme. Radios crackled; agents and informants came in and out of the command center. The place was controlled chaos, and I did my best to stay out of the way and keep quiet.

It turned out to be the largest investigation in U.S. history. I would later write the story with a colleague for *U.S. News & World Report*. The magazine put the story on its cover, and it apparently sold a lot of copies.

But that is not the point; the point is to treat leaked information with care and to be mindful of any lives or other risks that might be in play. The point is not the success of the operation, but the care that is taken with the information that has been leaked. One has a duty as a reporter to treat such information with utmost care. I tried to do that, and it worked out both for me and for the people involved in the investigation. That is the way the system should work.

# DO YOU HAVE A GUN?

## MAY 17, 2020

It is difficult to know why things happen the way they do around here.

This morning an elderly lady appeared at my door and asked, "Do you have a gun?"

"No, of course not. I don't believe in guns."

"What are you doing in here anyway?" asked the lady, who was dressed in a bright blue sweater and white slacks.

I gave her as brief a review of my medical history as one would give to a total stranger — that I was here in this rehabilitation center/nursing home to recover from a stroke so that I could get on with my life.

"Well, do you want to get out of here or not?" she asked. "Could we get through that doorway at the end of the hallway there?"

I told her that door was locked and armed with an alarm.

"That's why we need a gun," she said.

When I told her again that I didn't believe in guns she gave me a look of hopeless disgust and walked away.

The lady who has lived next door to me for months and who looks like a dyspeptic Albert Einstein, has suddenly disappeared. She lived quietly as a mouse most of the time, only exiting her room occasionally to unleash a barrage of obscenity-laden abuse on the staff. They moved her out yesterday because she had caught the Covid-19 virus.

Another man on the floor who I was friendly with for a while, Danny, has also disappeared. I am told he is in isolation because of Covid-19.

Well, that is one more for the virus and one less for us.

The other night there were two ladies crying on my floor — one on each end of the hallway. I had no idea why but there are any number of reasons why a person would cry here. Most importantly, people are not here by choice. Thus, many of us feel aggrieved and put upon. Any number of things that can happen to you

here would humble the stoutest of hearts. Most of us are clinging to any shred of dignity and respectability that we have left.

But the daily routine of institutional meals, bathroom visits, efforts to get in and out of the wheelchair can become overwhelming. It's hard to keep one's chin up.

We all have too much time on our hands, which is a recipe for trouble. I think that's why so many people here are so unhappy and susceptible to sickness, including from the Covid-19 virus.

I hear there are two entire floors of this four-story institution devoted entirely to Covid-19 patients. I have not been able to tally the exact number, but based on the number of residents per floor it must be pretty high.

A cheerful nurse's aide told me this morning, "It's bound to end sometime."

"I sure hope so," I said, "because we are running out of residents."

She didn't quite catch that, but I just smiled and let it go.

# MY DINNER WITH OLEG

Some time ago, I was asked to give a talk on the subject of international terrorism. The subject was dreadful, but the location was Paris, so how bad could it be? A friend of mine from Washington was also attending the conference and asked me to say hello to a friend of his whom I had not met before. The man's name was Oleg Kalugin, and he was a general in the Soviet KGB. For those of you not up on your John le Carré, the KGB are — or were — the true Russian heavies. Murder and mayhem only begin to top the list of their dark arts. They're also pretty good at upending opponents of the Politburo, fomenting foreign coups and winding up the odd piece of wet work in places like London and Tel Aviv.

To look at this quiet man sitting in a corner of a cozy café on the Left Bank, you would never know he had such dastardly deeds in his background. Built like a fireplug, he had a bullet-shaped head and ice-blue eyes. When my friend and I approached his table, General Kalugin was halfway through demolishing a delicate apple tart and had two glasses of what appeared to be a fine, old and doubtless expensive cognac in front of him. My friend, who was accustomed to me picking up his own expensive lunch tabs back in Washington, quietly explained that General Kalugin had come to Paris with precious little money to tide him through the conference. I understood immediately but was not put off. After all, how many times do you get the chance to buy a Soviet general a fancy dinner in Paris?

We proceeded to move from dessert to a thorough and thoroughly expensive wine list. What the hell, I thought, in for a dime, in for a dollar. By the time we got out of the café, it was damn near closing time and the conference had officially begun its second day. I didn't see General Kalugin again until I got back to Washington. I had been scheduled to do an appearance on a morning news show and the moment I stepped onto the TV stage, I spied the general across the room. He must have seen me at the same instant because the next thing I knew, he was striding briskly towards me. I had read somewhere that the general was scheduled to

testify before a Senate subcommittee on some POW-MIA issue dating back to the Vietnam War. I couldn't imagine what Oleg Kalugin would have known about POW-MIAs in Vietnam, but he was a KGB general so perhaps it was possible.

Anyway, I asked the good general what he was going to testify about when he met with the senators. He crinkled those ice-blue eyes and winked.

"I'm going to give them some *ledes!*"

# DECENCY AND BULLYING IN WASHINGTON

Among his many accomplishments before his elevation to the Oval Office, young Jack Kennedy published a slim volume in 1955 called *Profiles in Courage*. The then Senator Kennedy of Massachusetts profiled eight U.S. senators, men like Daniel Webster and Robert H. Taft, who through acts of bravery and integrity contributed to what we might call "making America great again" in their own day.

Casting an eye across the political landscape today it may seem hard to find examples of the type of courage that Mr. Kennedy profiled. But such people have always existed, often stepping into the limelight only in moments of crisis. In Kennedy's day, one need look no further than the famous Army-McCarthy hearings of 1954 and the testimony of Joseph Welch.

Senator Joseph McCarthy of Wisconsin was a bibulous political bigot who claimed to have found legions of Communists throughout the federal government. He would routinely claim to have lists in his pocket of every Communist working within the halls of the State Department. But there were no lists and precious few Communists. McCarthy was simply a bully.

A highly regarded Boston lawyer, Welch was hired by the Army to defend it against McCarthy's charges of lax security at a top-secret facility. At a hearing on June 9, 1954, McCarthy accused a young member of Welch's legal team of having ties to a Communist organization. Before a nationwide TV audience, Mr. Welch replied:

"Until this moment, Senator, I think I never really gauged your cruelty or your recklessness." When McCarthy tried to continue his attack, Welch angrily interrupted, "Let us not assassinate this lad further, Senator. You've done enough. Have you no sense of decency, sir, at long last? Have you left no sense of decency?"

The exchange effectively ended McCarthy's career and his reign of bullying. He died three years later at the age of 48.

The bullying that passes for political discourse in Washington has perhaps become more subtle in the seventy years since McCarthy, but it certainly continues to exist. And it continues to be resisted, sometimes in the headlines with much media fanfare and sometimes quietly in the background with acts of integrity that might have inspired Kennedy. I would argue that the latter case could be applied to the former FBI director, James Comey.

It may be lost in the mists of history now, but Comey's testing moment came late one night in March 2004 when he got a call from the chief of staff of Attorney General John Ashcroft, asking him to rush to Ashcroft's bedside at George Washington University Hospital in Washington. As Deputy Attorney General, the number two position in the U.S. Justice Department, Comey was serving as acting Attorney General while Ashcroft recovered from gallbladder surgery.

President George W. Bush had dispatched his two top aides to Ashcroft's hospital room to discuss a super-secret surveillance program run by the National Security Agency, the U.S. global eavesdropping entity. They wanted to discuss problems with the legality of the program. Comey was read into the program and knew all about the problems. Now he had to beat the two White House men to Ashcroft's hospital room.

At the hospital, Comey put his long legs to good use, striding up several flights of stairs to Ashcroft's room. Inside were members of Ashcroft's security detail and other FBI agents. Ashcroft's wife Janet, an accomplished lawyer like her husband, was also in the room. Comey had not been there more than five minutes when Alberto Gonzalez and Andrew Card burst into the room. Gonzalez was President Bush's White House Counsel, Card Bush's chief of staff. The two men said perfunctory hellos to Ashcroft then got into the surveillance program issues.

Ashcroft, with a herculean effort, propped himself up on both elbows in the hospital bed. He was suffering from acute pancreatitis, an extremely painful ailment that can in some cases be fatal. He listened to the two White House men, then gestured at Comey.

"I am not the Attorney General," he said. "There is the Attorney General."

It was the start of a battle between the Justice Department and President George W. Bush over whether Americans could be spied on without a warrant issued by a court. The surveillance program ended up being restructured largely because Comey, Mueller and the others stood firm, prepared to resign if the White House ignored the department's legal advice. A former federal prosecutor, deputy attorney general, FBI director and father of five, Mr. Comey clearly knew more than a little about loyalty, personal and professional.

Loyalty was the very quality that President Trump demanded of Mr. Comey when the two met privately over lunch in the White House Green Room. His refusal to offer that loyalty is what got him fired nearly a year ago.

Events seemed to have come full circle earlier this month when Mr. Comey's former deputy, Andrew McCabe, was fired as FBI director, days before his retirement. Mr. Trump celebrated McCabe's firing in a tweet, saying it was a "great day" for the FBI and that Mr. Comey made Mr. McCabe "look like a choirboy."

Mr. Comey tweeted back, "Mr. President, the American people will hear my story very soon. And they can judge for themselves who is honorable and who is not."

This is what the world watches and weighs today: who is honorable and who is not. Is the political bullying today coming from behind the desk in the Oval Office or, as the president's backers would have it, from "deep state" types like Mr. Comey and Mr. Mueller?

Mr. Welch's cry about "decency" in Washington seems as relevant today as it did in 1954. If JFK were around to do a modern sequel to *Profiles*, I think he would be watching very closely.

# JAMES COMEY

Throughout my career as a reporter and editor specializing in national security issues I have been interested in people like James Comey, who seem prepared to do the right thing even when the right thing is not at all obvious to many.

After reading an account in *The Washington Post* of the encounter in John Ashcroft's hospital room, I called Comey, who by then had left government service and was working for the Lockheed Martin corporation, a major defense contractor. I told Comey's secretary how much I admired what he had done in Ashcroft's hospital room and asked if he might be free for lunch. I had met Comey only once before and didn't know him well. Comey's secretary spoke to someone on the other end of the line, then said Comey would like to have lunch with me in the Lockheed Martin cafeteria.

I hastened over to his office in Bethesda, Maryland. This was not the lunch I had envisioned. I had planned on a quiet meal at a nice restaurant that would have allowed me to maybe get some interesting information from him (though Comey was no leaker). Instead, we were surrounded by noisy Lockheed Martin employees and privacy was impossible. Maybe that was Comey's intention in suggesting the cafeteria. I can't remember what either of us had for lunch that day, but I do recall Mr. Comey's quiet, unassuming demeanor.

Flash forward several months to the annual meeting of the White House Correspondents' Association. The dinner was a huge black-tie event and I was seated not far from Comey and his wife, Patrice. I had just written a book with a friend and colleague on the Justice Department's criminal division, and to my pleasant surprise Comey had a copy with him. In a self-consciously razzing tone he said to his wife, "That's the guy, that's the guy right there!"

I replied in mock horror, "Me? What did I do?"

Flipping through the book to the index in back, Comey showed me the offending passage. I had interviewed one of his deputies for the book, and the man

had had a heart attack before the interview and fallen off the low settee on which he had been sitting. When his body hit the floor, his heart restarted!

The index listed the man's name and two entries. One said "Died" and the other said "Returned from death."

Comey's finger stabbed at the offending words. He spoke to Patrice and to me.

"How can anyone manage something like that?" he asked, laughing. "How can anyone manage that?"

# SONGBIRDS
## JUNE 24, 2020

A few months back when the Covid-19 crisis first hit, I felt that I was in the eye of the storm. That is because I happen to live in a nursing home, not by choice but by necessity. And as we all know by now, nursing homes have been hardest hit by the virus, with an estimated 150,000 infections at 7,700 facilities nationwide.

My own facility has not been spared although the precise numbers are hard to pin down. The virus was first manifested here by the change in the appearance of the staff. Initially there were bandanas for face coverings, making the nurses and aides look like bandits. Lately there have been full-on hazmat suits, and the hallway procession outside my door has looked at times like the set of a *Star Wars* movie.

Recently some songbirds built a nest in a crack in our building just above my window and have been serenading me every morning. It leaves me with a great sense of peace and contentment.

The virus has not touched me directly, but it has gotten some of my fellow residents. My next-door neighbor, a lady in her 90s, caught the virus and was immediately moved to the second floor, where most of the Covid patients have been quarantined.

A man at the end of the hallway, who I had become friendly with, was also moved the second floor. Another friend, who had a room at the other end of the hallway, died of the virus. One of our nurses has also died and another has spent a period of time in an intensive care unit.

My family has not been allowed to visit in the four months since the virus first hit. Everyone has been affected in one way or another. One of my nieces has been furloughed from her job in Manhattan and the company is now abandoning its office lease, meaning employees will work from home on a permanent basis.

My nephews, who are either entering or making their way through law school

and business school, have no idea if they will have a campus to return to in the fall.

The songbirds keep chirping merrily, however, unaware of the crisis around them. Their song is like a tonic to my soul.

My only daughter lives far away in Michigan and I usually see her and her two small children once a year for the holidays. But we talk on the phone every day and she has given me a sense of how the crisis in playing out in the Midwest. She is doing OK but of course I worry about her and the children.

Last Christmas, she bet me that me that her little daughter would be up and walking before me. I took the bet and now it seems that Caroline has beaten me to the punch with plenty of time to spare.

# THE FALLUJAH PHOTO

Fallujah, Iraq, was by far the most dangerous place in a very dangerous country. Three American contractors, who should have known better but evidently did not, wandered into the city and were soon attacked by an angry mob of Shiite fundamentalists. Within minutes, their bodies had been burned and strung up on one of the city's main bridges.

A contract photographer, working for my magazine at the time, captured the image, and it was a powerful one. As the editor, I had to decide whether to run the image, or not. It was gruesome, grisly, perhaps unspeakably so. Photo editors on the magazine all argued for publishing the image. It was brutal and compelling, they said correctly, and it showed dramatically what war is all about, particularly war in a dangerous place like Iraq.

I anguished over the decision. This was something I would have to live with for a long time no matter what I did. There were the families of the victims to consider, for one thing. How would they feel seeing the image of their loved ones burned and hanging from a bridge? Of course, my magazine would not be the only one running the photo. It was too powerful for other publications not to run. And that, in fact, is precisely what happened.

I decided to run the image on the magazine's opening spread that week. *U.S. News & World Report* was not accustomed to getting lots of emails and texts, but before long I realized I had made the wrong decision. We were inundated with correspondence of all kinds, some, as I had feared, from the families of the victims, but most from just ordinary Americans outraged by what had been done to their fellow citizens by these Shiite fundamentalists.

Long after, I would read the memoirs of General James Mattis, who commanded the First Marine Division that would take control of Fallujah. General Mattis wrote that he would always charge his men to fight with a "clean conscience. Keep your conscience clean," he advised.

After the First Marine Division rolled into the city, Mattis followed and came upon one of his Marines making an arrest of some local Iraqis. Mattis inquired what the soldier was doing.

"Well, sir," the Marine replied, "we're taking the fun out of fundamentalism."

# MOZAMBIQUE

Before I went to Mozambique all I knew about it was that Bob Dylan had written the song "Mozambique," saying one could spend a week there. He did that just for the rhyme, I'm sure. I went for two months; I was sent by *U.S. News & World Report* to cover a civil war, a war that no sane person wanted anything to do with.

Instead of writing about the war I wound up writing about the kids who had been forced to serve as soldiers in the war. One in particular caught my attention. Frenice was a scared but brave little whip-thin boy with large almond eyes that captured my soul almost immediately.

I wrote a novel about my time in Mozambique called *Head Count.* In the book I described a terrorist campaign that was being waged against a fictional country, based on Mozambique, by its racist neighbor South Africa. The campaign involved depositing severed human heads in unfortunate and inopportune places around the country, places like the diving board of a hotel's swimming pool, a bus stop, you name it.

My entry point to Mozambique and to the kids fighting the terrible war there was the local Save the Children office. The woman running the office introduced me to Frenice and to some other boys equally brave and scared as he was. After I left Mozambique, I wrote to the woman several times, asking how the kids were doing, especially Frenice, who held a special place in my heart.

She didn't have much news about the boys, except for one thing: Frenice had last been seen paddling an unseaworthy wooden skiff out into the Indian Ocean by himself.

In my final, imaginary image, a slim figure soldiers on in a leaky old boat, alone, heading toward an empty horizon.

# THE DON'T KNOWS, THE PISSED OFFS AND THE SCREAMERS

## SEPTEMBER 6, 2020

The people in the place where I live can be divided into three very different groups.

The first are the residents who don't know why they're here or even where they are. I call them the Don't Knows. The second are those who know exactly where they are and why they're here and don't like it one bit. I call them the Pissed Offs.

The third group, considerably smaller than the first two, are the Screamers. These are residents who, by their own choice or not, scream or howl from morning to night. The Screamers can be drawn from both the Don't Knows and the Pissed Offs, which are represented, as much as can be determined, in roughly equal measure.

The Don't Knows and the Pissed Offs conduct themselves, in audiological terms, differently. The Don't Know screamers tend to be more tentative. The Pissed Off screamers, because they are well and truly pissed off, are more assertive and even brazen.

There are other sounds on the hallway as well.

The other night while walking with my aide Marie-Louise I thought I heard a small boy saying "Wow!" repeatedly.

I said, "Marie-Louise, have they started admitting children to Three South?"

"That's just Mrs. Quisenberry," Marie-Louise said. "She's got a respiratory ailment."

On days when the Screamers are in full cry I like to repair to the back patio, a beautiful place with abundant foliage and flowers in nearly all the colors of the rainbow. In this place I try to pull myself together and collect my thoughts.

"Don't respond to the Screamers," I tell myself. "It doesn't help."

Then I go back inside and ride the elevator up to Three South. In the corridor it is bedlam.

"Everybody, shut the hell up," I yell at the top my lungs. And suddenly Three South is as quiet as a graveyard.

"Wow!" says Mrs. Quisenberry from the door to her room.

I couldn't put it better myself.

# A MARVELOUS PIECE OF INSUBORDINATION

The guts of all great spy stories is counterintelligence. CI, as the spooks call it, lends all those elegant Le Carré novels and lurid Bond films their fine edge and supplies them with the patina of a well-drawn morality tale. Beneath all the hugger-mugger of the spy story, however, is a boring, even bland bureaucratic term: anomaly, which means something that doesn't fit into its surroundings.

When I heard that the FBI had arrested a spy deep within the CIA, I was immediately intrigued. The more I came to learn about Aldrich Hazen Ames, the more hooked I became.

Ames might have been the all-time king of anomalies. On a mid-level government bureaucrat's salary, he somehow managed to drive a cherry red Jaguar XJ6 sedan, live in a half-million-dollar home in one of Washington's toniest suburbs, pay for a live-in housekeeper, wear fine Italian suits and shoes—and the list went on.

As a reporter who covered both the FBI and the CIA for *U.S. News & World Report*, I had a peculiar, if not unique perch from which to view America's incestuous intelligence community. The Ames case gave me the chance to cover both agencies at the same time for one story. It was, I thought, the ultimate journalistic two-fer.

The first thing I did was to try and learn what the FBI might have on Ames. I found out where the case was being investigated, who was running it, and who was supervising it. The lead agent on the Ames investigation, which had been code named Nightmover, was Leslie G. Wiser, Jr., a former Navy lawyer and defense counsel. I got to know Wiser, and he was the antithesis of the classic G-man. He was not rock-jawed, stoic, and walk-through-walls adamant about things.

He was laconic, laid back, and easy to get along with.

He was also a spy hunter, pure and simple, and he was good at it. He proposed using a classic FBI investigative technique known as the trash cover, in which agents rifle trash cans left out on the public streets for pickup. But his supervisor, a genial good old boy named Robert "Bear" Bryant, demurred. Ames was a light sleeper, he said, prone to waking up at odd hours, and the trash cover technique was too risky. Bryant suspended the trash cover.

Wiser, in keeping with his profile of not being the classic G-man, promptly unsuspended the trash cover and soon found a critical piece of information that would lead to Ames's identification and arrest. Informed of Wiser's act, Bryant called it "a marvelous piece of insubordination."

In all, the KGB would pay Aldrich Ames some 4.6 million dollars for his efforts on their behalf, a sum I presume would have kept Mr. Ames in anomalies for many years to come. In the end, Les Wiser and his team of Nightmover agents amassed enough evidence to obtain a guilty plea from Ames, who would be sentenced to life in prison, and from his wife, who received 63 months.

I'm not sure how many hours I put in working the Ames case from both the FBI and the CIA angles, but it was quite a lot. It was my introduction to a classic counterintelligence investigation, and I would learn much about the two agencies I was assigned to cover, the people in them and how they went about their jobs. If it was on-the-job training, I thought, I would like to have more of it—a lot more.

# DEADLINES

The police scanner on the city desk crackled just before deadline. The rush of voices over the radio was rising quickly. One metro cruiser had slammed into another at an intersection. No one was hurt badly, just a few injured cops. Still, it was enough of an unusual occurrence to put it in the paper the next day.

The editor on duty barked, "Give it to Duffy, he's the fastest!"

I was also the youngest, just an intern, not even a full-fledged reporter. Nonetheless, someone shoved a yellow legal pad in my direction on the desk and I grabbed it frantically, listening at the same time to the chaos coming over the police scanner. Sirens shrieked; men screamed orders. There was some harsh background noise that I assumed might be a saw of some kind cutting through the wreckage of the patrol cars.

I wasn't sure what was going on and I didn't have time to figure it out, at least not much time. I started scribbling as fast as I could, listening for usable quotes. I wasn't sure of the ethics of using quotes that came over a police scanner, but felt without knowing for sure that if it was broadcast over a publicly heard medium it was fair game.

It must have taken only ten minutes to put the story together and it ran the next morning, stripped across the top of the Metro front. Our veteran police reporter, a woman who raised cats and carried a loaded .38 in her purse, was amazed at how quickly I'd written the story.

I tried to smile graciously. "Panic," I said, "is a wonderful motivator."

And so it was. Over the course of many years, I didn't have to worry much about such deadline pressures because I worked for a weekly news magazine, but when I got to NPR, a true 24-hour news machine, I felt the same adrenalin rush that I did that night on *The Miami Herald* city desk, combined with the added complication of always feeling that I was drowning in the deluge of non-stop news.

Deadlines, as I assumed everyone knew, are a fact of life for journalists. I was going to say an unfortunate fact of life, but I have found that deadlines have the effect of wonderfully concentrating the mind and forcing one to rule out everything that is not absolutely essential to the story to be told immediately. It is a great discipline, and one that, like so many things, can be learned only by doing.

Over the years, I would learn again and again the value of deadlines, and of writing long, sometimes complex stories under enormous deadline pressure. I'm glad to say I seldom failed to measure up to the test. I had an editor who was pleased every time I would be assigned to write a big story at *U.S. News & World Report*. When the owner called, as he so often did, to ask how we were handling a particular breaking new story, the editor, my boss, would say with a smile, "Oh, Duffy's on it. He's got the mighty Wurlitzer fired up!"

And so I did.

# THE MOANING MAN

## SEPTEMBER 13, 2020

Some things you just can't make up.

In the place where I am living there is a man down the hall who moans virtually all day long. Sometimes it is more like shrieks than moans — like the poor man is having his fingernails pulled out or suffering some other horrific torture.

I have asked the staff many times whether this man is really in pain or simply suffering from dementia. But of course, being a resident here I have no right to any information. Like Donald Trump with the coronavirus, the people who run this place believe that the best way to keep people calm is to tell them nothing.

I don't know if you have ever had the experience of listening to someone moan or cry or shriek for a very long time, but after a while it begins to get under your skin. And after a while you begin to want to start shrieking yourself: "Shut the hell up and give the rest us some peace, will you please?"

To my shame I admit to having done this more than once.

Being the inveterate reporter that I am, I refused to submit to this management "no information" policy and went to my own sources. One of my best is the Hispanic custodian, Manny, who is in and out of every room with a mop every day and knows everything.

"Manny, is this guy really in pain or is he just gaga?" I asked, accompanying the question with a twirling finger motion by my head because Manny, whose English is approximative, did not seem to immediately seem to understand the word "gaga."

"Oh, he is in much pain," Manny said, shaking his head. "He has a plastic tube…." Manny struggled for the word.

"A catheter?" I suggested.

"Yes, a catheter which enters his belly and giving him much pain."

I later stole down the hallway in my wheelchair to have a look at The Moaning Man myself. He was quiet for the moment, but he lay crumpled on the bed like a

piece of paper and his face was a mask of pain.

I mumbled an apology for my tirades, but the words seemed hollow.

Some things you wish you could make up after all.

# THANK YOU, MR. MADISON

He was a mite of a man, the height and weight of a jockey. To his fellow Founders, though, James Madison was a giant, both intellectually and morally (though, like many of them, he owned enslaved people). A complex and complicated man, Madison was never more so than on the question of press freedom.

On one hand, his writings are littered with profuse references to a "lying and licentious press." On the other, press freedom was among the first of the nineteen amendments he drafted personally to the original Constitution. What to make, then, of Madison on the press?

Madison, as his several biographers have noted, was particular about the historical record, especially as it referred to himself. He was, as the historian Garry Wills notes, forever doctoring the public record as it pertained to himself.

Perhaps his views of the press can be attributed to little more than his concern for propriety in the affairs of state, but is it not more likely that Madison was concerned about how history would portray him, based on his own writings and what was being said about him in the writings of others?

The press in Madison's time was far different than it is now. During the Revolutionary War and in the eight years of Madison's presidency the press was notorious for attacking figures in the public domain. Headlines were often sensational and littered with references to personal and even sexual taboos; insults and terms of opprobrium were commonplace in the pages of newspapers and magazines. Could it be that Madison worried about a press that felt it was free to shoot from the hip on matters of personal decorum or decency? Maybe he had good reason to fear the freedoms of the press, particularly as they referred to himself.

Despite his reservations, Madison believed that freedom of the press was an essential element of a liberal democracy. As he wrote in 1800: "To the press alone, checkered as it is with abuses, the world is indebted for all the triumphs which have been gained by reason and humanity, over error and oppression…"

That is good enough for me and it should be good enough for everyone else. Thank you, Mr. Madison.

# MADISON, JEFFERSON, AND NPR DRIVEWAY MOMENTS

It probably goes without saying, but working in a newsroom for a broadcast medium like radio or TV is significantly different than working in a newsroom for a print publication like a newspaper or magazine. The differences involve much more than the level of ambient noise, although that is a factor.

As a refugee from the legacy print media, I had mixed emotions about coming to NPR. I was uncertain about giving up life as an ink-stained wretch to try a new job in broadcasting.

When I took the position at NPR a friend said, "Well, Duffy, it looks like you finally made it, man. Plus, you have a perfect face for radio!"

Perfect face or not, there were things about the new job that made me smile. The combined audiences of NPR's two big daily news shows, "Morning Edition" and "All Things Considered," was greater than the combined circulations of every American daily newspaper and news magazine.

My days at NPR were long. Each day started before "Morning Edition" went on the air at 5:00 a.m. and lasted well into the night, long after "All Things Considered." As I made my way through the day at NPR, the news programming would be broadcast over the in-house public address system, and I would listen with great care. I wanted to ensure that the stories I had been involved with as a reporter or editor were being voiced and presented in the way we had agreed in our earlier story meetings in the studio.

At NPR the two big news shows dominated the programming, but information was presented throughout the day that I had a hand in either developing or reporting. I listened most days with my heart in my mouth because I had not been a broadcast person and was learning on the job.

At NPR we had things that my colleagues referred to as “driveway moments,” stories so compelling that a driver would reach their destination but stay in the car listening, not turning off the engine until they heard the end of the piece.

James Madison and Thomas Jefferson both wrote eloquently about the need for informed citizens in a robust democracy. At NPR, I felt as if we were affirming that observation while at the same time making good on its implied promise. No one reached as many Americans with the level of informed, educational content as we did at NPR. Many of us at NPR despised the word “content,” but that is what the media provide, and the more informed the content, and the more integrity it has, the more likely it is to make good on the age-old admonitions of Madison and Jefferson.

# THE DAYROOM AND MUHAMMAD ALI

There's a room in the place where I live that I almost never go into, despite the pleasant shafts of buttery sunlight coming in from the windows on three sides. The staff refers to it as the dayroom.

Evidently, the dayroom was initially intended as a place where residents who needed greater supervision or help in their daily tasks could be overseen by a smaller group of staff.

As in any place that caters to the aged or the infirm, the ratio of staff to residents is a key metric of success or failure. At this odd junction in our history, togetherness — although considered an admirable goal in general — is frowned upon. Nevertheless, the needs of the residents in this room are such that several aides must be present all the time.

No one ever says it, but this room seems to have been reserved for residents suffering from Parkinson's and Alzheimer's disease. The reason I seldom visit this room has nothing to do with the people in it but more because the TV is kept on day and night so that the golden light from outside must compete with the blue light from the TV. On most days the blue light wins.

It may seem odd to talk about a heavyweight boxing champion in the context of an old age and rehabilitation facility, but it occurred to me that some of the people in this room might benefit from hearing about a visit I once made to Muhammad Ali.

In 2001 *U.S. News* arranged for me to interview Ali on his farm in southern Michigan. I was struck, as many had been, by his warmth and sense of humor.

The Champ stepped out of the front door and lit up with a big smile. The 1,000-watt smile was still there, I could see. And underneath the loose pullover that he wore, the massive shoulders were surely still there.

The Parkinson's disease that afflicted him for more than a decade had robbed Ali of his fancy footwork and made speaking difficult. But he did his best to choke

out the words and I did my best to understand him.

I had read up on Ali's epic bouts, including the "Thrilla in Manilla" against Joe Frazier in 1975. I had also watched all of his equally famous interviews with sportscaster Howard Cosell, where the two men bantered and where Ali made his famous remark that he "floated like a butterfly and stung like a bee."

He still had the ability to float and sting, I saw, even if his words tumbled out of his mouth in semi-coherent fashion. There was no denying that the brain was still there, it's just that the words came out a little garbled.

And the Champ, there was no doubt, was still the Champ. He talked a little more and we walked over to the barn with his wife Lonnie, his chief advocate and principal fan.

"This," Ali said, pointing to a regulation size ring he had constructed in the barn of his farm, "is where I work out."

Lonnie laughed, in a kindly way. "When he's not talking, he means," she said. We all laughed at that, including their son, Assad, who was maybe three or four years old.

Ali, in addition to his many other accomplishments, was a supremely funny man.

It was not just the "float-like-a butterfly-sting-like-a-bee" catch phrases and the comic doggerel that he would bandy about in sports interviews, but humor pervaded his view of the world. It seemed to be his way of saying — as with Parkinson's disease — "that life can be tough, but you just can't give in to it."

Stories have been told about Ali's friendship with comedian Billy Crystal. In one such tale, Ali and Crystal were attending Howard Cosell's funeral.

Ali said to Crystal as the service droned on, "Little brother, do you think he's wearing his hairpiece?"

"I don't think so," Crystal replied.

"Well then how will God recognize him?" Ali asked.

"Champ, once he opens his mouth, God will know," Crystal said.

Ali recalled many such stories on the day of my visit as we strolled about to check on his plantings. I brought up, as a reporter must, Ali's refusal to serve in Vietnam and famous declaration that: "I ain't got no quarrel with no Vietcong."

He said the opprobrium heaped upon him for that decision didn't trouble him. "None of it bothered me at all," he told me. "God was with me."

The visit concluded on a gentle note of friendship with Ali signing not one but two pair of boxing gloves for me, which I in turn would give to my two godsons, Sean and Brian. I protested a bit but not too much. After all, these gloves would be a memento of a life that had been lived in the full glare of the world's attention, if not its understanding.

Ali feinted one more punch and I again pretended to stagger backwards.

"Gotcha," he said.

And the interview was over.

# A $175,000 BEEMER IN BAGHDAD

The flaws of the Second Iraq War have been amply documented, so there's no need for embroidery here. By placing a dollar sign on my modest involvement as a chronicler of that war I do not mean at all to minimize the sacrifices of those who lost much more than money.

The $175,000 mentioned above is the price I paid for an armored BMW to chauffeur the reporters and photographers I had dispatched from Washington to cover the conflict. We bought this high-priced German beauty in Mexico and had it shipped to Baghdad. I won't even get into what that cost. But to preserve my guys and gals from experiencing the worst of that hellish conflict, I thought an armored car was the least I could do.

On the plane to Baghdad the pilot announced as we were approaching the airport that we would be making an unusual descent. Unusual didn't quite describe it. As we approached the airport the pilot pushed the Boeing 737 into a nearly vertical dive.

This type of landing, we learned later, was to avoid being shot down by a missile.

The insane landing did nothing for either my heart or my digestion. On the ground we were met by two British special forces veterans we had recruited to provide security for our house in Baghdad. They had the Beemer and a second armored Mercedes, which we were going to use as a backup car should the first one run into trouble.

We would be traveling to the house, the Brits told us in their clipped accents, at an altitude of ½ inch off the ground and a speed of 90 to 100 miles an hour. The NASCAR craziness was necessary, they said, to avoid the random gunfire that plagued travelers between the airport and Baghdad's Green Zone.

We didn't quite escape the gunfire, however. When we got to the house, we discovered a slug in one of the laptops stowed in the trunk of the armored BMW.

The Mercedes escaped unscathed. That was as close as I hoped to get to any gunfire during my sojourn in Baghdad.

One of our more enterprising reporters had arranged for the magazine to rent office space in downtown Baghdad not far from the Green Zone perimeter. A bunch of other foreign press were in the same building, one of Baghdad's more disreputable hotels, which I guess is why they didn't mind letting foreign reporters crash in their rooms and hallways.

The parking for this establishment was underneath the building. The office space we had commandeered was on the third floor and there was a decent place to eat and drink a few floors above us.

For entertainment, we sat on the roof and watched the missiles and tracers score the night sky over the city. Of course, Saddam Hussein's artillery knew the location of the hotel that housed the despised foreign press, so it was not exactly an accident when a day or two after our arrival a missile scored a direct hit on the hotel. There were many casualties, though far fewer than if the attack had occurred at night, because most reporters and photographers were away from the hotel doing their jobs. Our *U.S. News* crew were staying at the house we had rented near the U.S. Embassy so none of us were hurt.

At that point, I'd be surprised if we had put more than three or four miles on that beautiful BMW. When the building collapsed, the Beemer and the Benz were crushed beyond repair. If memory serves, the total loss was well over $300,000.

War is hell, and it's not cheap, either. It can be made up of individual accounts of courage and cowardice but in the main it is the story of sadness and sorrow. And, of course, loss.

# IT HAPPENS ALL THE TIME

It was stifling hot Saturday and I rolled down the window of my little rented Renault. Soon a rock flew through the open window and missed my head by inches. As I drove, more rocks, along with bottles and other assorted items, came fast and furiously.

I hightailed it down the storied hill from Jerusalem back to Ben Gurion International Airport. I had come to East Jerusalem with a colleague to report on the Palestinian Liberation Organization. We wanted to understand why the PLO had lost the affections of the Palestinian people it had held for so long.

The PLO seemed to have been replaced in the hearts of many Palestinians by Hamas and, to a lesser extent, by Hezbollah, the Shiite Muslim political party and militant group based in Lebanon. We wanted to know why.

By the time I got to the airport all the windows of my Renault that had not been rolled down were smashed out, allowing the lovely Mediterranean Sea breeze to blow through the open car.

When I pulled into the rental agency car return, the man behind the counter said: "Don't worry, sir. It happens all the time."

# ISOLATION KILLS, MR. CUOMO!
## SEPTEMBER 22, 2020

The latest bulletin from HQ came in this week with, as usual, new instructions for us on the front lines. Now we are told, all visitors must produce a negative Covid-19 test each time they arrive, or they won't get in the front door.

This injunction, like all the others, is supposed to keep us safe. We are all for safety but as the bulletins and injunctions and instructions have begun to pile up, you wonder if they are starting to do more harm than good.

I often get the feeling that these orders are coming from our Supreme Allied Commander, which for us in New York, is Governor Andrew Cuomo.

Since the pandemic erupted in New York in March, Mr. Cuomo has striven mightily to beat it back and crush the infection curve. And he has largely succeeded, by relying on science and data and by being persistent. And in a move appreciated by many New Yorkers, he updated the electorate with the facts every day at noon.

So he's a hero right? Not where I live, which happens to be in a nursing home in New York State. Mention the governor's name to any doctor, nurse, aide or administration person inside this place and you immediately meet hostility. In here, Mr. Cuomo is despised.

"He screwed things up royally," my therapist, a kind man who works hard to get me back up on my feet, told me the other day.

The hostility stems from Mr. Cuomo's interaction with nursing homes early in the pandemic.

On March 25, fearing that Covid patients could overwhelm the hospitals, Mr. Cuomo issued an order that required nursing homes to accept Covid patients being discharged from hospitals as long as they were "medically stable." Nursing homes receiving the patients were barred from testing them to see if they were still contagious.

Dozens of New York nursing homes didn't see their first Covid-19 case until

they were forced to comply with Mr. Cuomo's order. Over the succeeding months, 6% of the state's nursing home population, or roughly 6,500 residents, died. On May 10, Mr. Cuomo rescinded the order.

I bring this up not to indict Mr. Cuomo. There are no paradigms for how to operate a nursing home in the midst of a pandemic. You get the best scientific advice you can, and you do your best.

I bring it up to point to another danger. Now that nursing homes have become the Ground Zero of the pandemic, regulators are falling over themselves to protect us. The result is more and more bureaucracy and residents becoming more and more isolated, and the frailest among them dying.

AARP recently warned of "a mental health crisis" in nursing homes caused by "loneliness, abandonment, despair and fear" that was pushing the death toll from the virus much higher.

Mr. Cuomo, we know that you want to keep us safe but frankly all your injunctions from HQ to the front lines are driving us crazy. Our families can't visit. Even simple things like getting a haircut or a manicure have become impossible. But the worst of it is the isolation, which is killing almost as surely as the virus.

# A SHORTAGE OF WORKERS

## SEPTEMBER 21, 2021

My shower nights are Wednesdays and Sundays but this week there was no shower. I was told it was due to a shortness of staff.

Living in a nursing home, my situation is far from unique.

According to a June survey by the American Health Care Association and National Center for Assisted Living, 94% of nursing home providers had a shortage of staff members that month.

It's a hard job and the low wages don't justify the risk. And the risk is real, both for residents and workers.

As of June 13, Covid-19 has killed 132,000 U.S. nursing home residents and 1,900 staff members, according to the Centers for Medicare & Medicaid Services.

U.S. nursing homes and residential care facilities employed 3 million people in July, 380,000 fewer than in February 2020, according to Bureau of Labor Statistics data.

*The New York Times* has reported that staff shortages in some homes have gotten so bad, those with severe dementia are being given antipsychotic drugs to keep them calm.

In that context missing an occasional shower is not a big deal.

I don't know if the place I am in is using antipsychotic drugs to deal with its worker shortage. Frankly, there are so many nutty people here it would be difficult for me to tell one way or another.

The other day, my next-door neighbor, a lady who is either 91 or 96, she can't remember which, asked me if I had my ticket. She seemed to believe that we were all on an airplane headed off somewhere.

"No," I said. "I don't have a ticket."

"Then what are we supposed to do?" she asked.

"I don't know," I said. "I guess we'll figure that out when we land."

# DEMENTIA AND ITS AFTERMATH

In his beautiful, if unorthodox, biography of the 40th U.S. president, *Dutch: A Memoir of Ronald Reagan*, Edmund Morris adopts a peculiar narrative style, inserting himself in the role of "imaginary narrator." Early in the book, Morris suggests he knows that there is "something wrong" with Ronald Reagan, but not until much later do we see Reagan beset by cognitive confusion, which during his second term evolved into full-blown dementia and Alzheimer's disease.

According to a congressional investigation, before his second term was out Reagan had approved the sale of military hardware to Iranian mullahs in exchange for the release of hostages they were holding in Lebanon, and the use of those profits to bankroll Contra rebels fighting the Sandinista government in Nicaragua. Some observers believed that because of his Alzheimer's disease, Reagan was not fully aware of having engaged in those transactions.

The disease continued to progress until the point where he received a diagnosis confirming that he had Alzheimer's. After consulting with his wife Nancy, Reagan decided to handwrite a two-page letter to the American people informing them of his diagnosis.

"I have begun the last journey that will take me into the sunset of my life," Reagan wrote. "But I know that the American people will always have a bright dawn."

As a reporter working for *U.S. News & World Report* in Washington I covered the Iran-Contra scandal, and I remember the jokes some reporters were exchanging with congressional staff investigators.

"What did the president forget and when did he forget it?" went one joke.

Today, I see no humor in the subject of dementia. I live in a nursing home surrounded by people suffering from the disease. One man in my hallway asks me repeatedly each day where his room is. Each time I give him the same reply, pointing out that it is the same room he had the day before and the day before that and that his name is next to the door.

Another man wandered into my room the other night as I was listening to the Reagan biography. I had never seen him before. He was thin almost to the point of emaciation, and he clearly did not know where he was. I told him he was in the wrong room, but he proceeded to sit down anyway and to stare vacantly at the floor.

*The New York Times* recently published a piece on Dianne Feinstein, the 88-year-old Democratic senator from California. The senator has had an illustrious career in politics, distinguishing herself in the Congress with several committee chairmanships, most recently on the Senate Judiciary Committee. Sadly, Senator Feinstein has recently become the subject of a whisper campaign suggesting that she can no longer remember details of conversations and other interactions she has during the course of her day. Suggestions have been made openly that she should no longer continue to serve in the Senate.

I am neither a Democrat nor a Republican, but I know from a long period of covering politics as a journalist, and now from living in a place where dementia is the rule rather than the exception, that casting dementia patients aside is clearly not the answer.

Public figures like former President Reagan and Senator Feinstein have the ability to put the scourge of dementia squarely in front of the American people so they can do something about it. Raising awareness, raising money for research, keeping people with mild cases of dementia in the mainstream as long as possible – those are steps that may lead to breakthroughs in treatment.

Shunting people who are capable of taking care of themselves into "memory care units" where they are out of sight and out of mind helps no one.

# THE MOST DIFFICULT STORY

It was every parent's worst nightmare. You take your kid to a crowded mall, he slips away, and somehow falls into the hands of not just any killer, but a killer straight out of the horrific tabloid headlines. This was the story of young Adam Walsh from Hollywood, Florida.

In the Fort Lauderdale newsroom of *The Miami Herald*, I was given the assignment to write about young Adam's ordeal at the hands of two serial killers, Henry Lee Lucas and Ottis Toole. You could hardly have invented two worse specimens of humanity for Adam to have encountered. They decapitated him then mutilated the body, buried it in a shallow grave, and dared police to find it.

*The Miami Herald* is a highly respected and dignified newspaper, but in covering the Adam Walsh case I felt as I might have been writing for *The New York Post*, or worse, *The Spectator* or *National Enquirer*. The details are almost too ghastly to mention.

Lucas was a serial murderer from Texas who claimed to have killed so many people that the Texas Rangers who interviewed him after his arrest soon concluded that he was making up names and identities. Toole was, if anything, even worse. A pyromaniac who had lost one eye, he had become Lucas's lover. They traveled the country together, doing roofing jobs and moving from town to town in a desultory killing spree that defied the imaginations of even hard-eyed detectives charged with solving the crimes.

A lede-all, in the parlance of journalism, is a story that often runs on the front page of newspapers that must accommodate news developments reported by several different reporters from multiple angles. On the Adam Walsh case, I was assigned to write the lede-all each day, and it soon became the subject of macabre jokes among the reporters working the story, such as how much I'd relish writing the term "one-eyed pyromaniac lover." But I took no delight in writing such things. I felt terrible that Adam had suffered so atrociously at the hands of these two scumbags.

Yes, I said it. Toole and Lucas were two scumbags with no redeeming social value, and they deserved anything they might have coming to them. Death would be a merciful outcome, I thought. Put the sons of bitches out of their misery.

Many reporters have the occasion to write about murders during the course of their careers, but the Walsh case was by far the worst I ever had to cover. It was a subject of abject sorrow and horror. How could there be such evil in the world? How did it fall on the slender shoulders of little Adam?

I found no answers to these questions. During the several weeks when I had to cover the Walsh case and write about it every day, I learned from my family that a neighbor's daughter had killed herself back home by setting herself on fire after she learned she had become pregnant.

My wife at the time and I regularly attended Mass at a small church not far from the newspaper office, and I went there one day to ask the priest to say a prayer not only for my neighbor's daughter, but for Adam Walsh and his mother and father so that their terrible pain might somehow be eased. I did not know if that was even possible, but I believed that if it *were* possible, only God might be able to lift such a burden.

# THE HIGHLIGHT OF THE GAME

## JANUARY 16, 2020

There are a lot of bad things about old-age homes, as any resident will tell you. Probably the worst thing, however, is that the days are long.

Real long.

The better old-age homes usually have a team of people to organize recreational activities for the residents, but that is not always the case. Sometimes the residents have to organize the activities themselves.

The residents of the home where I live organized a balloon volleyball tournament. On the face of it, this might seem absurd because a balloon cannot fly through the air like a ball. It floats. And who should be surprised by that? That is what balloons do after all.

The good thing about the floating balloon is that it moved slowly enough so that the geriatric residents could gather themselves under it and with their feeble reflexes try to hit it over the net to the other team. The game would go back and forth this way for a short time, 20 minutes or so, until one team gave up or a winner was declared.

During one game recently, the lady next to me, in a reclining bed, hit the balloon up towards the light fixture and it exploded when it struck the hot light bulb. The lady in front of me, a kindly woman, who strolled the hallways at night with a caftan around her shoulders, gave a cry — whether of delight or alarm I am not sure.

Her name is Emilia and is a timid soul who bothers no one and expects the same in return.

The balloon hitter in the reclining bed had been a guitarist in an all-female band in Chicago, and when the balloon popped she barked something at Emilia that I didn't quite catch. Emilia, taken aback by what the ex-folk singer had said to her, responded in kind and a new match—a foul-mouthed slanging match—was underway.

This surprised me. I had never heard Emilia speak like that before and didn't know that she was capable of such language.

In any case, the depleted balloon was stuck on the ceiling and refused to come down. That led to a series of accusations and counter-accusations between the ex-folk singer and Emilia. Neither would give an inch. Finally, one of the girls from the recreation department who had been observing the game blessedly intervened. The ex-folk singer, she said, should not have yelled at Emilia. She had done nothing wrong, and certainly had done nothing to cause the balloon to pop.

Eventually, cooler heads prevailed. The game concluded with one side or the other winning, I can't remember which. All that anyone could seem to remember after the game was the unlikely shouting match between Emilia and the ex-folk singer. That was easily the highlight of our game.

# BREAKING BABY NEWS

The phone rang just as I was running out the door to work, and I grabbed it. For a journalist a ringing phone always means the possibility of breaking news, the rubric that seemed to run my life and rule my workday.

This *was* breaking news, of a different kind: breaking baby news! The pleasant voice on the other end of the line said, "We had a beautiful baby girl born here. Can you and your wife be here tomorrow morning at nine?"

We could and we were. My wife and I had been unable to have children of our own, so we had decided to adopt a child.

When we entered the agency in Tampa, Florida, we found our daughter exactly as the lady had said: a beautiful baby girl. She looked up at us with big round eyes and a sweet smile. I melted immediately. So did my wife.

We spoke with the baby's mother, who explained that she had several other children and could not afford to raise another.

We flew back to Washington, D.C., where I had moved from Florida to take a job at *U.S. News & World Report*. This was not only a move for me to the big stage of the nation's capital, but a move from daily print journalism to a weekly newsmagazine, another beast entirely. Theoretically, the change should have been a breeze. Instead of the daily deadlines of a newspaper I would have a whole week to get things done. That seemed simple enough, but I soon learned that I would need to develop some little literary tricks to make a story I wrote a week ago seem fresh when people got the magazine in their hands. It was not just banging out copy without thinking or reflection.

Not long after we returned to Washington my wife and I, sadly, divorced, and flying became something of a theme in my daughter's and my life together. Katie moved with her mother to Michigan while I stayed in Washington. I remember many days standing in airports after putting her on a flight to Michigan by herself, looking out at the empty tarmac where her plane had just been, and sobbing.

Flying also played a happy role in our lives. On weeks when I would go to Michigan to see Katie, if there was nothing to do we would fly west across Lake Michigan to Chicago and take in a play or a ball game or a movie, or just walk around the city and enjoy the gorgeous architecture, walk along the river or the lakefront, visit the Shedd Aquarium or the Art Institute. The city had endless attractions, and we got to nearly all of them.

We took other plane trips as well. I was an avid skier and was determined that Katie would learn the sport at a young age. She was three years old when I first got her up on skis, and we didn't do the bunny hill, either. Out west we skied Colorado and Utah; back east we skied Vermont, and favored the Currier and Ives town of Stowe, far north near the Canadian border.

On one occasion in Utah, I bought her a full-day lesson. At the end of the day, her instructor motioned to me and I skied over. Instead of asking for the payment, as I had supposed, he told me, "Now, sir, you're going to hear the three scariest words you'll ever hear on a mountain." He looked meaningfully at Katie, standing on her skis a bit farther down the slope.

"Dad," my daughter called out, "follow me!"

And follow I did, or tried to. Katie was skiing like a little demon under the trees, while I was having difficulty ducking low-hanging boughs. Her legs pumped like pistons as she navigated one mogul after another, while I had to slow down to avoid getting my clock cleaned by a low branch. By the time I got to the bottom I was out of breath and scared that Katie would not be there waiting for me, but there she was, grinning like the little imp she was.

It wasn't just ski trips. One time we went to the Bahamas and saw the attractions of Atlantis. Katie and I swam with dolphins, and we still have photos of us looking uncertain and alarmed in the water next to this big, beautiful gray mammal.

We went to London once. That was probably our biggest trip, and it was Katie's first time overseas. At our hotel I had requested a room with a cot, and what they gave us was a room with a huge, four-poster canopy bed and a little Lilliputian cot pushed into a corner. Katie, naturally, got the big bed and I got the cot.

We visited the bunker where Winston Churchill had managed the Second World War as prime minister, and saw the cot he had slept on while German bombs fell during the Battle of Britain. I noticed with some interest that Sir Winston's cot was not all that much larger than mine at the hotel.

I remember walking along the streets near our hotel and hearing all the different languages being spoken: Chinese, Russian, Spanish, French, Italian and more. We took a famous black London taxicab, and before I could say a word the driver asked, "Where to, guvnah?" Katie remembers that to this day, maybe her first memory of being overseas.

One time in Washington, Katie and I met a colleague for a quick sail on the Chesapeake. My colleague brought along her beau, who had an important job with one of the intelligence agencies. I covered intelligence, and my colleague made me promise that I would not ask him any unseemly questions. But we had not been in the boat five minutes when Katie made polite small talk and asked him, "So, Joel, what do you do?"!

Eventually, we would get two English cocker spaniels from a breeder that Katie found in Tennessee, so that was one more trip. Katie, remembering London, named the male Winston and the female, for some reason, Chloe. I guess that's as good an English name as any, even if it originally was Greek.

As the years went on, Katie would ask me time and again why her mother had given her up for adoption. I told her the truth. "Your mother loved you so much that she wanted to give you a better life than she could give you herself, so she put you up for adoption. It was probably the hardest and most painful decision she ever had to make, but she did it because she loved you, not because she didn't love you."

In time, work would so fill my head with news stories and stuff I had to remember for my job that I felt as if I had no more room in there, but then Katie had a family of her own, and soon I had to make space for an impossibly pretty little girl with a beautiful smile like her mother's, and a strong, handsome big brother with a shock of black hair and a smile that could stop traffic.

Recently, Katie delighted me with news I never expected. She is going back to school to get her college degree. When Katie was small, I took her and her

cousins to see *The Lion King* on Broadway, and I still remember that beautiful song from the play, "The Circle of Life." With her decision to return to school, Katie is completing another turn on the circle of life, and her kids will surely be the beneficiaries of that turn, as I will, too, one of these days.

You go, Katie. There's no stopping you now, honey.

All my love,

Dad

# COVID BEAN COUNTING

## FEBRUARY 22, 2021

The place where I live is not very big as such things go, just three stories and room enough for some two hundred souls.

This reflection is prompted by the latest statement from New York Governor Andrew Cuomo about the number of people in the state's nursing homes who died from Covid-19.

The New York State Attorney General issued a report recently saying that the number may have been undercounted by 50%.

Fifty percent is a pretty large number no matter how you cut it, but Governor Cuomo said it was not so. He said the numbers had been reported "fully, promptly and accurately." But in the next breath, Cuomo said he took responsibility for any failure that may have resulted in the numbers not being reported either fully, promptly or accurately.

It is hard to know what to make of such statements.

The only thing that I can say as someone who has lived through the pandemic in a nursing home is that the confusion, or lack of transparency if you will, is understandable.

Of the three floors here, one entire floor was devoted to Covid patients. These were people who were infected, or who might have been exposed, or who had just come from the hospital or who were on their way back to the hospital. There was a constant shuffling in and out as nursing home operators tried to respond to the latest directives from Albany.

As you can well imagine, many of these "patients," old, frail, with serious health issues, simply died in the shuffle. Whether they fell through the cracks in Albany's accounting or were deliberately miscounted for political reasons is not for me to say.

What is clear from my point of view as an "insider" was that we in New York were overwhelmed last year at this time by the pandemic. Systems that should

have been in place to protect vulnerable communities from rapidly spreading infectious diseases were not in place. These are the questions that our public health officials should answer.

The rest, how many died and where they died and what they died of precisely, is just so much bean counting.

# YOU CAN'T FIRE ME, I QUIT

It is not well remembered now, but not long after the 9/11 terrorist attacks, news organizations were warned about suspicious pieces of mail turning up in their mailrooms containing a mysterious white powder. The first one arrived at the *National Enquirer* offices in Florida, followed soon after by pieces of mysterious mail sent to *Time* magazine and CNN. At *U.S. News & World Report* magazine where I was working, we had one suspicious piece of mail show up in the New York office.

"It's an insertion order," an employee said.

That surely was suspicious. An insertion order is an order from an advertiser to insert an advertisement in the pages of the magazine. Because of incursions the Internet had been making on legacy print media, *U.S. News*, like so many print publications, had been receiving fewer and fewer insertion orders. Advertisers had found they could buy online ads that would precisely target the specific group of consumers they wanted to direct their ads to, so they preferred an online buy to a buy in a print publication like *U.S. News*. And online buys were far cheaper: in *The New York Times* a single page advertisement could cost as much as $50,000.

Because the online buys were so much more attractive than buying ads in a print publication, many advertisers had shifted their ad dollars to the Web and had abandoned print media like *U.S. News.* The situation was even worse for newspapers. They had lost a substantial source of revenue in the form of classified advertisingrevenue. Websites like Angie's List and even Facebook listed all kinds of merchandise for sale and other things that used to be advertised in the classified ad pages of the newspapers.

One day I woke up in my new home and felt like I had a hole in my stomach. I had recently gotten divorced and just bought a new house, though it wasn't exactly new—it had been built in 1929, perhaps not the most auspicious of years, but it was mine and I owned it, or at least the bank did and let me live in it.

But that wasn't why I had a hole in my stomach. I was the editor of *U.S. News & World Report*, and aside from the responsibility of publishing a weekly newsmagazine and managing an editorial staff of some one hundred journalists, including reporters, writers, editors, photographers, researchers, even a library staff, I had to manage a budget, and that was the problem.

The man who owned the magazine was constantly after me to cut the budget. I knew the budget could not be cut without cutting the staff, which I refused to do. I had hired many of those people myself.

So I practiced my line over and over again. "You can't fire me," I said to myself. "I quit." The more I said it, the more I liked the sound of it. "You can't fire me, I quit."

Then one day I actually did decide to quit. I walked out of my new home and over to Wisconsin Avenue, one of the big north-south thoroughfares in Washington, D.C., and decided to walk all the way to the office on the other side of the city. Except that I would not go to the office first. I would go to see my friend Gloria Borger, then working at CBS News, not far from where my office was. On the way I stopped and called the man who published our magazine and told him that I was resigning. I had had enough of the pressure, I said, and would not fire the people they wanted me to fire. I refused, pure and simple.

That done, I continued walking to my friend's office. When I got there, I told her flat-out that I had just resigned. She was a good friend and reassured me that I had done the right thing. I still felt sort of numb, however, right thing or not.

I finally went into the office and told the people there that I had quit. Everyone had different things to say, but I kept repeating my mantra to myself: You can't fire me, I quit.

It still sounded pretty good to me.

# A ROGUES' GALLERY
## FEBRUARY 22, 2021

When you live in places like the ones I have been in during the last few years, some people leave an impression. A rogues' gallery if you will.

In the first place there was a man who was gruff but fun to talk to. He had worked, or so he told me, as a fisherman, running a trawler up and down the New England coast.

The man's boat was 87 feet long and he was either 92 or 93 years old, he couldn't remember which. He also couldn't remember why he was in the place or when, if ever, he was getting out.

The rumor up and down the hallways was that he had a problem with drink and his family put him in rehab to give his poor liver a rest.

He would seek me out every day for some reason and we would chat, usually in the coffee room. He liked telling fishing stories and tales of the sea and I like listening.

I started referring to him as the Ancient Mariner and eventually I came to know him by no other name.

Another character in this place was an Afghani woman who paced the hallways in her hijab, smiling kindly and seemingly interested in all her fellow residents. She liked me because I took the trouble to learn and pronounce her Muslim name.

After a while, however, I received another view of this woman. This view came from another resident, a woman who had lived in Manhattan and was in the rehab center because she tripped over her cat and broke her leg. The cat, a rescue animal, seemed like a monstrous beast the way she described it, but she said she loved it and couldn't wait to get back home to it.

Anyway, I said that this Afghani woman seemed to have a good soul and my cat-loving friend arched her eyebrows and shot back: "She does not."

The woman said that all the smiling and touring up and down the hallways was a ruse. In reality, this woman was looking for the chance to creep into other residents' rooms and rifle through their things. She apparently did not steal but liked to inspect all the meager items that residents kept in their small rooms. In her room, my Manhattan friend said, she had committed the cardinal sin of over-watering her orchid, thereby killing it.

You would think that in these kinds of places, full of the old and frail and the sick, that people would be treated with a certain gentle care, a certain kindness. I am here to tell you that ain't the case.

There is a man on my floor, who is also my friend, who has a tattoo of a skull and crossbones on his arm and he seems to find the old and the frail very amusing. His own ailment is somewhat mysterious, but it keeps him in a wheelchair.

Whenever an Alzheimer's patient makes too much noise or a hard-of-hearing resident plays the TV too loud, Mr. Skull and Crossbones can be heard bellowing in the hallway.

"Turn it down, Big Ears!"

Then he typically has a big laugh as he rolls on down the hall to the nurses' station where he usually tries to cadge a cigarette or two.

# PANDEMIC FATIGUE

## MARCH 2, 2021

Ordinarily, nursing homes are among the sleepiest places in the world. Today, sadly, this is no longer so. In the place where I live, the doctors, nurses and aides patrol the corridors with masks and bandanas over their mouths looking like Wild West bank robbers.

The danger has nothing to do with flying bullets, however.

Less than 1% of America's population lives in long-term care facilities, but they account for 34% of all U.S. coronavirus deaths. That amounts to 175,000 deaths in nearly 35,000 facilities.

A second source of concern other than simply staying alive is the mental toll that the virus and the isolation normally associated with it are causing among those who live in long-term care.

Some doctors have taken to calling this "pandemic fatigue." Many elderly residents suffer from various forms of dementia and the isolation and loneliness from not having family visits certainly makes this worse.

We have one woman here who patrols the hallways calling for her mother, father, sister, baby son and young daughter, not necessarily in that order. It is hard to say for certain how old this woman might be but judging from her appearance, if her mother and father are still living, they are probably older than God.

Another neighbor of mine, who recently turned 91, had forgotten altogether that she had a daughter although the woman who is now in her 60's came to visit regularly before the pandemic.

One evening as I was sitting in my room after dinner, I heard the lady who was seeking her parents and her children start a conversation with my neighbor. It might have been an amusing conversation were it not so sad.

The woman accused my neighbor of having her husband in her room and demanded that she return him immediately. My neighbor protested that she did not have any person like her husband in her room, but the lady still demanded that

my neighbor release the man immediately.

My neighbor continued to protest that she had no such person in her room. The lady who had been searching for her parents and her children became unhinged.

"Police!" she called in a shrill voice. "Police!"

# A "FUCK YOU MOMENT" WITH THE MIGHTY DRAGON

When U.S. Defense Secretary Robert Gates visited Beijing in 2011, he was greeted like visiting royalty, or to put it in democratic terms, like a real president. Gates' stay had all the trappings of a state visit, and his meetings with the Chinese leadership went more or less as planned—at least until senior officials of the People's Liberation Army rolled out a model of their new J-20 stealth fighter, also known as Mighty Dragon. That, according to an aide traveling with Gates, was a real "fuck you moment."

Gates told his hosts in Beijing that the American press would undoubtedly begin writing and talking about the rollout of the J-20, and said he could not be held responsible for what they might say or write. Gates' comments about the press were in the tradition of many American leaders traveling abroad to discuss foreign policy.

When President-elect Donald J. Trump interviewed his choice for secretary of state, Rex Tillerson, Tillerson told him that U.S. leaders had four aces to play when dealing with foreign governments: the American economy, the American military, America's freedoms, and American democracy. Tillerson himself was not the greatest champion of the First Amendment, by any means, nor was he a notable beneficiary of the freedoms it espoused and guaranteed the American press, but it is notable that he listed press freedom as among the most important elements of U.S. foreign policy negotiations.

America, of course, has long been known around the world for the liberties enjoyed by its citizens, including the press and entertainment industries. American movies and television programs are regularly transmitted around the globe and attract audiences in the hundreds of millions worldwide. The freedom of the Amer-

ican press is something else entirely, however. Leaders everywhere on earth have experienced the passions, pride and prejudice of the American press, and understand its power and influence all too well. The American press seldom pulls its punches, and when it thinks it has found a bully that needs bloodying or a tyrant that needs taunting, it does not hold back.

Some presidents, like Mr. Trump, have taken to belittling and berating the American press for its excesses, or in Donald Trump's case, for its presumed partiality to mendacity. For all his glib talk of fake news, Mr. Trump was as aware of the power of the American press as any President, perhaps even more so.

In books written by American journalists about Mr. Trump, including several by *Washington Post* writer Bob Woodward, Mr. Trump says that he feels compelled to engage with reporters "because he loves it so much." It is as if he cannot help himself, or perhaps more likely, it is because he cannot stop talking about himself. In any case, the allegation of fake news is unworthy of further discussion.

Not so, however, the assertion of Mr. Gates in Beijing about the power of the American press. The American press has a peculiar, almost unique power in the world. Its powers are regularly debated by the Supreme Court, and on a less elevated level, by politicians and political figures like Mr. Gates. That power is real, as many foreign leaders have found to their chagrin. When the American press exercises that power it tends to constrain what those leaders do, and perhaps worse from their perspective, allows their citizens to see that happen.

At the end of Secretary Gates' trip to China he found himself, according to his memoir, *Duty*, wondering if the rollout of the stealth fighter during his visit was really a "fuck you moment," or whether perhaps officials of the PLA had decided to roll it out of their own volition, without consulting the political leadership. That, Mr. Gates writes, would have been far more worrisome. Every government, it seems, may have its wild card, whether it be a rogue press or a rogue military.

# THE SADDEST ACRE IN AMERICA

Humam Khalil Abu-Mulal al-Balawi didn't look like your typical Al-Qaeda terrorist. One of the few known pictures of him shows the young Jordanian in a starched white shirt, dark suit coat and dark tie. He is clean shaven with closely cropped, neatly parted hair. It might be a picture from a yearbook or perhaps a driver's license.

Al-Balawi studied medicine for six years in Turkey at Istanbul University and graduated in 2002. He also received medical training at the University of Jordan Hospital and at the Islamic hospital run by Jordan's Islamic Brotherhood in Amman. He was married to a Turkish journalist and translator, with whom he had two children.

But Al-Balawi was an Al-Qaeda terrorist and had become an asset of the Jordanian intelligence service. The CIA wanted him as a spy too, but when agency officials tried to arrange for Al-Balawi to bring them to Osama bin Laden and his second in command, Ayman al-Zawahiri, they found that because the Jordanians had Al-Balawi first they controlled his movements in Pakistan.

Unfortunately, Al-Balawi was a double-agent, pretending to work for the Jordanians and the CIA but still loyal to Islamist extremists.

A meeting was set for 30 December 2009 at a CIA facility operating inside a forward military base near the Afghan city of Khost. The car carrying Al-Belawi was driven by the chief of external security at the base and was waved through three checkpoints without stopping. When it arrived at 4:30 P.M., 16 people were waiting before the building that had been set aside for the debriefing. Before Al-Belawi even emerged from the car he detonated a suicide vest, killing himself, seven CIA officers and one Jordanian officer.

It was the second-worst day in terms of casualties in the CIA's history, exceeded only by the attack on the U.S. embassy in Beirut in 1983.

Among the dead CIA officers was a cousin of my fiancée, Mary Beth. After

the tragedy, Mary Beth and I went to Arlington National Cemetery several times to visit Elizabeth's grave. She had been interred in Section 60, reserved for Americans who had died in the wars in Iraq and Afghanistan. Section 60 has been called "the saddest acre in America."

After Elizabeth and her colleagues were buried there it became sadder still.

The death of young people, I suppose, will always be a cost of war. But it hits home so much harder when a person killed by a suicide bomb half a world away turns out to be a family member.

# THE UNIFORM OF MY COUNTRY

I have never been privileged to wear the uniform of my country, but I hold those who do and did in the highest respect and regard. So when I came to write a book about the first Iraq War, I did so with no small amount of unease and anxiety. Who was I, with no military experience and no ability to analyze military affairs, to second guess those who had dedicated their lives to that pursuit?

I had covered national security issues, but only from the perspective of the FBI and the CIA. I had friends in both agencies and respected them and their dedication to their fields. Still, it was something else again to write about people who literally made their livings under fire, and to judge decisions made by them under pressure and often with limited or inadequate information.

With a friend and colleague, I wrote a book called *Triumph Without Victory*. The title alone suggests a strong element of judgment. That was based on our review of the stated purposes of the generals who ran the war, General H. Norman Schwarzkopf, leader of the United States Central Command, and General Colin Powell, the Chairman of the Joint Chiefs of Staff.

General Schwarzkopf had been quoted as saying that a principal objective of the war was the destruction of Iraq's elite Republican Guard. In the course of the war, however, the Republican Guard was not destroyed.

Well, objectives are often unmet in every human endeavor, so why was this different? My co-author, a former naval officer, and I decided this was different because America had encouraged Iraq's Shiite and Kurdish minorities to rise up against Saddam Hussein, and when his Republican Guard units were not destroyed, they were instrumental in putting down those rebellions. America's word had been on the line. We had encouraged the Shiites and Kurds to stand up to Saddam, and when they did so we allowed them to be crushed, precisely because the objective of the war, as stated by its commander, had been unmet.

Considering my high regard for members of the U.S. armed forces, I felt un-

easy about the judgments that we made in the book. Nevertheless, I stand by them, and I know my co-author does as well. There is no finer calling than to serve one's country, and to put one's life on the line for duty and honor. I respect that enormously, but when the job goes undone it is the journalist's job to point out that fact, with no malice or attitude attached to that judgment. That is the way I did my job, and that is the way I would expect the people about whom I wrote to do their job if they were judging me.

Turnabout, as they say, is fair play, and that's all I am interested in.

# UNDERDOGS: WAR AND BASKETBALL

It is an obscenity, on many levels, to make comparisons between a sporting event, like a basketball game, and a military atrocity like the ongoing Russian invasion of Ukraine. Games like basketball may inflate and enervate spectators but are quickly forgotten, while war represents a far more durable and exacting tally of success and failure.

Nevertheless, such comparisons may be instructive. Americans, for instance, have an instinctive preference for underdogs, ever since throwing in their lot against George III. They will root hard for a Cinderella team like the St. Peter's Peacocks from Jersey City, even as they send money and clothing, food and other necessities to residents of the ravaged cities of Ukraine.

Those, like Valdimir Putin, who fail to understand this do so at their peril.

On the hardwood, the peril is less meaningful, of course. There a talented underdog like the Peacocks may go into a full court press and run their opponents off the floor. In Ukraine, the cities pummeled by bombs and rockets have revealed populations that show remarkable resistance, hope and courage. They have held, and in some cases even pushed back the Russian advance, even in the most hard-hit places like the besieged port of Mariupol.

Parallels between such wildly different subjects may sound fatuous but they illuminate important truths and values like the importance of courage, of conscience and, if it is not too corny to say so, fair play.

So "Go Peacocks!" "Go Ukraine!"

# SARKIS AND SADDAM

Few reporters are lucky enough to report both ends of a truly bizarre story separated by many years and many thousands of miles. I did just that and here is how it happened.

When I started out as a cub reporter in Miami, I didn't know my foot from first base, but I quickly heard about a fabulously wealthy Lebanese arms dealer who lived on a billionaire's island in Biscayne Bay, escorted starlets to splashy parties and flew choppers almost everywhere, whether he was in a hurry or not. He strutted the stage of his life like a cartoonish Croesus. Everyone in the newsroom wanted a shot at Sarkis Soghanalian, or at least his story. I only got the latter some years later.

I eventually moved to Washington D.C. to work for *U.S. News & World Report*, where I specialized in national security reporting and wound up writing a book with a friend and colleague about the first Iraq war. During the research for that book, we discovered that the same Sarkis Soghanalian had sold a bunch of Blackhawk attack helicopters to Saddam Hussein.

At *U.S. News* I was asked to write a cover story about Saddam titled "The Most Dangerous Man in the World." I learned that Sarkis had been indicted by the Feds in Miami and sent to a local jail in the Florida panhandle. Crime was so rampant in south Florida that the authorities had run out of federal jail space, so they sent Sarkis to this podunk hoosegow in the hinterlands.

I traveled back down to Florida and drove across the panhandle to try and locate Sarkis. When I found him, the man who had supplied Saddam Hussein with the fearsome Blackhawk attack helicopters was padding liked a caged tiger around a tiny cell in the back of the lockup.

I told the jailers I had come to interview Sarkis, and after some negotiating, they brought him out to see me. Sarkis introduced me to Bobby, his "taster," the only remnant of his once vast retinue. The former hotshot Lebanese arms dealer

feared being poisoned in this smalltime slammer and had brought along Bobby to taste his food before he ate it.

I had hoped that Sarkis could give me some insights into Saddam's personality and help me to understand a bit more about the Iraqi military. Unfortunately, though Sarkis proved to be gracious and hospitable, he was unable to tell me anything I needed. After an inconclusive chat of perhaps twenty minutes, Bobby chiming in with inane remarks whenever the conversation stalled, Sarkis escorted me outside the jail. In the rearview mirror of my small rental car I saw a patrician's wave, as if he owned the place.

The book about the Iraq war was eventually written and we called it *Triumph Without Victory*. I think we included Sarkis in the book, but he played only a minor role. He was not a big fish in the overall story, certainly not on the order of Saddam himself.

That's sometimes how journalism works. You get different pieces of a story at different times, then have to put them all together to make a coherent narrative.

That's what happened with Sarkis and Saddam. It worked out pretty well in the end, at least for me. Sarkis and Saddam would undoubtedly have a different opinion.

# LIZARDS UNDER MY DOOR

## FEBRUARY 10, 2022

I have three little green lizards that live under my door. They are cute and move only when I look at them. Their big brother, however, is not quite so cute. He is about the size of an alligator, and lives under the laundry cart in the hall just outside my room. He scares the bejesus out of me.

I have a tight tangle of spiders who live in my toilet bowl. They move all the time, twisting and turning in the bowl and roiling the water as I sit on the seat.

The spiders and the lizards, I am told, are the product of my having been over-prescribed one of the several antidepressants I am on. Like most of the residents in this nursing home, I am old (though 67 is much younger than most people here) and infirm after a stroke took away the use of my left arm (I'm left-handed) and caused me to walk with a limp, and only with assistance.

Most of us here have little to be happy about and less to look forward to. We are trying to cling to any last shreds of dignity we may have left. In my case, that is precious little indeed. This is close to hell as I ever hope to get.

# MARY BETH

In the place where I live, it is hard not to conclude that I am knocking on a closed door, that I have, in short, hit bottom.

I moved to this nursing home after the woman I had been living with for twenty years was diagnosed with cancer and died. This was after I had had a stroke that crippled my left side and left me unable to walk unaided. I have only realized since coming to this nursing home that for much or most of the time Mary Beth and I were together, she was probably dying. Realizing that fact now, however belatedly, has added to the depression that has descended on me, for which I take several powerful antidepressants.

But this is not about me. This is about Mary Beth, and specifically about the classy way she ended her life. Because of my stroke, I was unable to do much of anything to help her in the small apartment we shared, but she never uttered a word of complaint or unhappiness. Instead, no matter how poorly she may have been feeling, Mary Beth made sure that I got out of our apartment almost every day to walk. Walking is the best therapy for stroke victims trying to recover what they have lost.

On bad days, when it was cloudy or rainy, Mary Beth would take me to walk at Annapolis General Hospital, where I had been in outpatient therapy. A doctor there had told us that the upper floor of the hospital was not occupied and that outpatients could go up there to walk.

On good days, when the weather was nice, Mary Beth would take me to the Naval Academy Bridge, not far from our apartment. There we would often share a deli sandwich on a weathered picnic table on a beach before she took me to walk on the old bridge, which had been abandoned to make way for the new one and converted into a fishing pier, stretching out over the gray-green chop of the Severn River.

As I limped out toward the end of the pier, Mary Beth slowed to match me

stride for stride. The pier was populated most days by a number of old Black men fishing for blue crabs, and we would stop to talk with them. Mary Beth, like any good Marylander, knew that to catch crabs you need chicken necks or other parts of a chicken, so she never asked the fishermen what they were using for bait.

Instead, she unfailingly asked the old men how they liked their crabs cooked. Mary Beth didn't need any recipes. She knew every way under the sun how to cook Maryland crabs, and then some. She just loved talking to people, especially people she had just met and with whom she might have little in common. As we talked to these old Black fishermen, I could see them sizing the two of us up and wondering what this crippled little white guy was doing with this beautiful blonde woman. I'm sure Mary Beth noticed the same thing because she never missed much of anything, but she was too polite to say so.

Mary Beth and I never married, but it was not for my lack of trying. I asked her three times to marry me, and despite the old saw, the third time was definitely not the charm. Instead, she gave me the ring of her favorite aunt, her Aunt Katie. It was the commitment ring Katie wore when she became a nun. I have it to this day, and it is one of my most prized possessions.

Before Mary Beth and I moved in together, and before I had my stroke, I had been a reporter for several newspapers, including *The Wall Street Journal* and *The Washington Post,* and for a national newsmagazine, *U.S. News & World Report.* That's where I met Mary Beth. She worked on the business side of the magazine, and when we went out with my journalist friends, she was always quick to point out that she was not a reporter or a journalist.

"No," I would quickly chime in, "Mary Beth, has a real job." That always brought a laugh to her which delighted me. I loved to see her laugh.

I owe Mary Beth more than I can say for all she did for me during what until then was the most difficult time of my life. (Now is even harder, living without her.) Mary Beth approached everything in life with an endearing mixture of passion and impatience. I will give you an example. I came to this nursing home where I live because I understood that the therapy offered here was superior to the therapy offered at other nursing homes, but when I got here the pandemic had hit, and the nursing home suffered a shortage of trained staff, like so many other

healthcare facilities. The director of therapy here said that for me to learn to walk again, I need to be walked at least twice a day by the nurses' aides, but now that almost never happens.

In my inner ear I can hear Mary Beth responding to the nursing home operators. "Well," she would say, "if you don't have enough staff, you will simply have to get more staff to help Brian walk." And that is the way she would say it, too—with no intemperance, no poor language, no invective. Just a straight factual assessment of the situation and a straight factual assessment of how to rectify it. That was Mary Beth to a T. I was the journalist, but she was the one who was the "Just the facts, ma'am" type of person.

I have been trying to make myself write every day on my blog, but it's not easy. A lot of people with dementia live here, many of whom seem to think of my little room as the place to congregate at any time of day or night.

Again, I can hear Mary Beth's voice urging me to do better.

"You can do it, Brian. Ignore all the noise and the people with dementia. You can *do* it. Now *do* it!"

Mary Beth's voice in my ear, and her commitment to helping me walk again, are the things I remember most about her, and why I love her so much and miss her so terribly. I have managed to finish this piece only because I hear Mary Beth's voice telling me to wrap it up and be done with it.

OK, Mary Beth, I'm done now.

All my love,

Brian

# NIGHTTIME SOUNDS IN A NURSING HOME

During the night on my darkened corridor, things sound much different than they do in the daytime.

On one end, an engineer with several patents to his name cries for help in a hoarse, helpless voice. Nearby, an old woman who seldom speaks above a whisper during the day, yells at someone in angry, agitated tones.

Somewhere, a slow, strangled "No!" echoes down the hall.

Nighttime sounds in a nursing home, where dementia is the rule rather than the exception.

During the pandemic, the risk of Covid infection has been the greatest worry in nursing homes, particularly for those who own and run them. But for those of us who must live in them the toll has been immeasurably greater.

The virus has shattered many of the family connections that seemed to keep a lot of my fellow residents from tipping over the edge. As the staff has focused on masks and injections the mental health toll has gone largely unnoticed.

It may be years before the full scope of the mental damage from the virus is fully known. In the meantime, we all are doing our best to cope with the strain.

# A BRIEF ENCOUNTER WITH MADAM SECRETARY

Honoring someone for a job well done can lead to the most intimate human connections, but for my money, it is better as an utterly impersonal act.

This thought came courtesy of a late-night news bulletin reporting the death of former Secretary of State Madeleine K. Albright. I did not have the privilege of knowing Secretary Albright, but she presented me with an award for some reporting I did with a colleague at *U.S. News & World Report* on the Palestinian Liberation Organization.

My colleague was an Egyptian woman who had covered the tumult of the Middle East for many years and knew her way around the PLO and its factions. Together, we looked at financial ledgers in London, spoke to political partisans and professors in Paris and – most importantly – invested some serious shoe leather reporting in the West Bank.

The piece examined what had gone wrong with the PLO. Why had it lost its long-held purchase on the beleaguered Palestinians for whom it had advocated for so many years? Why had Hamas, designated by Israel as a terrorist organization, eaten the PLO's lunch? What had caused PLO Chairman Yasser Arafat and his lieutenants to take their eye off the ball?

After a fitful start, a clear and concise narrative began to emerge from the reporting. The problems of the Palestinians were all too well known: grinding poverty, endemic violence, weak family structures. In its early years, the PLO had sought to address those problems and more. It had established community organizations at the street level, hospitals, clinics, legal aid offices. But then, somehow, mysteriously, they gave it all up.

Why?

My colleague and I sought to answer the questions and found some suggestions in the dozens of people we talked to. Somehow, no one could quite articulate the reasons for the PLO's failure. Had the organization and its leaders become tired? Had they lost their revolutionary zeal? Was the whole struggle just all too difficult?

There were profound questions, and we would not find many easy answers.

From their protected perch on this side of the Atlantic, many Americans thought that the PLO's problems stemmed from its embrace of political violence. My colleague and I examined this premise carefully and found that evidence for it was underwhelming. The PLO had been associated with terrorist acts over the years, and it had been blamed for many others by Israel and its advocates, but evidence for the PLO as a sponsor or advocate of violence was minimal.

Secretary Albright expressed her delight at having read such an interesting article. On her staff were a number of distinguished Middle East experts including the former U.S. ambassador to Israel and special envoy to the region, Martin Indyk. That she and they had appreciated our effort made the weeks of hard work worthwhile.

During the brief ceremony at which Secretary Albright presented the award, she complimented us kindly on the research and analysis we presented in the piece. I thanked her for her kind words and soon the transaction was over. That, in my judgment, is precisely how such transactions should be conducted.

Thank you, Madam Secretary. May flights of angels guide thee to thy rest.

# A VERY COVID CHRISTMAS

## DECEMBER 24, 2020

I know that all of you out there in the great, wide world are plenty sick of Covid and the seemingly endless, pain-in-the-ass pandemic. I get it.

And for those of us who have been closed in nursing homes since before the pandemic began, and in some cases long before, we are facing yet another Covid Christmas and it is no fun. No fun at all, dammit!

We all remember celebrating the holidays in better places, I am sure, but for pure depression, few things match celebrating the nativity of Our Lord in a nursing home and singing "O Holy Night" and "The First Noel" to your fellow residents.

Speaking of those residents, why have empty beds and empty rooms suddenly begun to appear again on our hallways, and why are friends and neighbors again starting to disappear, seemingly vanishing into the night?

Victims of the dreaded virus? Did they go to a hospital? Hospice care? No one knows for sure. And if they know they sure are not telling us.

In New York where I live such questions are often hard to answer because Covid cases are shuffled back and forth from hospitals to nursing homes to the point where it is impossible to get any straight accounting of the situation. This has caused no end of distress to me and my fellow residents because we would like to know what happened to those friends and neighbors we cared about who are no longer here.

Christmas is a day away and a winter storm is due to hit right on time for Rudolph to lead the other reindeer and Santa's sleigh. The closest any of us in this place will come to any of that is the toy reindeer antlers that many staff members have taken to wearing. It makes the nurses and aides look kind of cute, but that, too, reminds us of how far we all are from living a normal life.

So, all you Christmas merrymakers out there, have a wonderful holiday, and try to spare a thought for those of us who are stuck in places like this one.

Merry Christmas and best wishes for a better New Year!

# MY LATEST SCOOP

Over the years much has been written about Yasir Arafat, much of it inaccurate, some, sadly, not uninfected by animus.

To his Israeli interlocutors, the long-time chairman of the Palestinian Liberation Organization was a nervy negotiator and an implausible partner for peace who had been dealt a bad hand by history and who had contrived to play it badly.

To members of the Western press, who covered his global peregrinations in Palestine's cause, he was, above all, a creature of the night. For reasons known only to Arafat, he deigned to give his rare interviews to correspondents only several minutes before or after midnight.

Thus it was that a friend then covering the PLO chairman was invited, and appeared at the appointed hour for the late-night colloquy only to be told that the great man was occupied and that she must wait.

Killing time, my friend sat with a bunch of burly bodyguards outside Arafat's chamber watching old cartoons on a small black and white TV. When Tom and Jerry flashed on the screen a big man sidled up to my reporter friend and said:

"So, who do you like? Tom or Jerry?"

Such either-or propositions are not uncommon in a land where faith, fossil fuels and geography combine in a combustible brew that often explodes in bitter anger and antagonisms, some of which may last millennia.

In a place where time can take her own sweet time, she can also be surprisingly swift, and even light on her feet. In 1967 an Israeli army, having been caught flat-footed by armies of three of its Arab neighbors, soon routed the interlopers and carved a new slice of sand out for the state of Israel and drastically redrew the boundaries of the Middle East.

The war was over in 72 hours. Then it fell to another man whom history had dealt a bad hand to pick up the pieces on the Middle East chessboard and set them aright.

Henry Kissinger was a German Jew who lost thirteen family members to the Holocaust, earned a Ph.D. from Harvard, then went to work for President Nixon as his National Security adviser and later Secretary of State. It was in that latter capacity that Dr. Kissinger accepted President Nixon's letter of resignation, then flew off to the Middle East to see about setting things right there.

In classic Kissinger fashion, he saw the complex questions of the region with uncanny clarity. First, he said, all disputants, but especially the Arabs, must be assigned defensible borders so they would not be tempted to cross those of others and reignite the fighting. Second, Moscow's big commissar's boot must be removed from the region once and for all. Third, and most important to Kissinger personally given his faith and family history, Israel must be guaranteed a survivable identity in a very rough neighborhood.

This may have been a more daunting challenge than even Dr. Kissinger had imagined, but he had not made his reputation as a global dealmaker by tackling small problems. Even so, the problem may have been even more complicated by the fact that in creating the Jewish state in 1949 and seizing on the British Mandate for Palestine to do so, the United Nations chose the homeland of the peoples of ancient Palestine, and from that decision would flow years of recriminations and unlooked-for results that have echoed down the years long after Henry Kissinger left the world stage.

Much of this history has been well and ably told by journalists and historians, but not all. As a reporter for *U.S. News & World Report* in Washington D.C., I had covered the Central Intelligence Agency for many years. But it was not until after I left Washington and returned to New York to live with my family that I made a surprise discovery, courtesy of a man who had worked for the CIA.

He didn't know that I had been a reporter and that I had covered the CIA, but one morning at a gathering of neighbors on a quiet beach, he began speaking of Israeli prime minister David Ben-Gurion and the CIA. Interested, I eased over to sit next to him.

The man told me he had worked for the CIA for many years and had intimate knowledge of its intentions and operations in the Middle East. A cousin of his, he said, had recruited Mr. Ben-Gurion as an asset, or source for the CIA, at the precise

time that Dr. Kissinger was conducting his historic negotiations after the 1967 War.

That information has not previously been disclosed. It is reported here for the first time.

Printed in the USA
CPSIA information can be obtained
at www.ICGtesting.com
LVHW082037041123
762998LV00035B/1200/J

9 781662 941009